Missing Men in Education

Missing Men in Education

*Mary Thornton and
Patricia Bricheno*

Trentham Books

Stoke on Trent, UK and Sterling, USA

Trentham Books Limited

Westview House	22883 Quicksilver Drive
734 London Road	Sterling
Oakhill	VA 20166-2012
Stoke on Trent	USA
Staffordshire	
England ST4 5NP	

First published 2006

British Library Cataloguing-in-Publication Data
A catalogue record for this book is available from the
British Library

ISBN-10: 1-85856-344-5
ISBN-13: 978-1-85856-344-2

Designed and typeset by Trentham Print Design Ltd., Chester
and printed in Great Britain by Cromwell Press Ltd, Wiltshire.

Contents

Introduction

How can we understand men who teach in our advanced, 21st century society? From our sociological/social psychological perspective, teachers, are constructed like all members of society, as gendered, classed, raced and aged people. Our task is to understand these gendered patterns, to understand how people position themselves within such patterning and to open up possibilities for change by identifying sites that operate to control or empower us.

We argue that gender is a social construction (chapter 2), that as individuals we develop masculine or feminine identities through our life-long experiences and interrelations with others in social settings. Our gender is neither determined at birth nor fixed by any particular experience or event. Rather, it is complex and changing, depending on the context and circumstances in which we live and the degree of agency we are able and willing to exert in our lives. As individuals we exhibit infinite variety in our gender identities.

Nevertheless, as groups of men and women living within particular times and social/cultural contexts, gender patterns emerge. A variety of types of masculinity and femininity can be identified within these more general gender patterns, with hegemonic masculinity (Connell, 1995) being the term that we use to describe the dominant and most structurally powerful form of masculinity to be found within our society today. It is not an easy concept to define because it is largely based on being not feminine or female but it does include stereotypes of male behaviour such as competitiveness, aggression, assertiveness, dominance and power. Such traits contrast sharply with stereotypes of femininity such as co-operation, subservience, conformity, subordination and lack of power and ambition. We will highlight the complexity and constraints such concepts of masculinity and femininity impose on men considering entering education.

Are we 'missing men' in education?

We are certainly missing men in terms of the numbers who teach. Teaching is a gendered occupation; there are far more women teachers than there are men. Where men do enter teaching, they are largely missing from the classroom chalk face, since they disproportionately occupy management positions. If they stay in the classroom they are liable to be addressed as 'miss' by children, given their routine experience of women as their teachers, in much the same way that young children sometimes call teacher 'mum'.

Whether or not men are missed from teaching is a different question, requiring thoughtful debate and empirical evidence rather than political assertion and rhetoric. The absence of men from the lives of many children in single parent families is blamed for all sorts of things, raging from laddish behaviour and discipline problems, through anti-academic approaches to compulsory schooling, into street violence and abusive relationships. The prescribed remedy is more men as teachers to provide positive male role models for children. But this assumes that children see their teachers as role models – which on the whole they don't – and that there is an agreed, desired style of male behaviour that men as teachers should model, which there is not. Female single parents tend to want male teachers to model stereotypical male characteristics for their fatherless boys, of sporting prowess, toughness and discipline, not an interest in poetry or art. Arnie Schwarzenegger in *Kindergarten Cop* exemplifies this mind set (Weber and Mitchell, 1995).

We may also be missing men as targets for recruitment to teaching because new entrants must have work experience with children, or because of the representation of teaching, especially of young children, as akin to mothering and therefore more natural for women, or its presentation as a low status and relatively low-paid profession. We also fail to recruit men through the prevalent assumption that men wanting to work with children are either paedophiles or gay.

This book goes beyond the knee-jerk reactions of media, politicians and popular commonsense perceptions, in order to enhance our understanding of why men are missing from education, what roles and responsibilities they take when present and whether or not their absence matters to children, schools and society at large.

Men and boys are subject to far greater public scrutiny now than ever before. Being male is now a public issue. Hegemonic masculinity, manifest in laddish, anti-academic behaviour, is set against the image of caring new men who nurture children and eschew traditional stereotypes. At the same time, the concept of teaching as mothering has been superseded by government policies that favour more masculine traits such as heightened discipline, competitive testing, inspection regimes and centrally prescribed curriculum structures. In the chapters that follow, we explore the contradictions that surround men who teach, how they have developed and changed over time.

Research perspective

For some academics the research that underpins the arguments presented in this book will be seen as perpetuating a positivist view of gender and teaching. We reject this. Patterns and tendencies are identified: to deny them would be to ignore our social history and the societal structures which shape us all. The point in identifying them is to demonstrate that they are not fixed in stone. They are social and historical constructs that can be changed, albeit not easily or quickly. As individuals and groups we are shaped by many things: our class, race, culture, family, friends, abilities, experiences, and our time and place of living. We are also shaped by our gender. There is as much variation between individual men and individual women as there is between men and women as distinct social groups. The patterns we identify are snapshots of a particular time and place, not *a priori* truths about men who teach. Ours is a social-constructivist perspective (Moore, 2000:32) which seeks to understand the structures that constrain us better to make space for their re-negotiation and re-configuration and thus alternative ways of being men and women in education.

Over the past ten years we have interviewed, surveyed, researched and analysed men who teach. It has been an iterative process between engagement with the literature, engagement with policy issues and debates, data collection and analysis, conversations with others and re-engagement with literature. Brief methodological outlines for the main research projects on which our data are based are given in appendices. Like all researchers we strive to be value-neutral, and have adopted 'a grounded approach, using rigorous methods such as triangulation and feeding back results to research participants' (Greenbank, 2003:798). However, we also accept that research can never be totally value free. What the data tell us depends on what questions we have asked, the context in which they were asked, and the nature and perspective of the questioners.

Sargent (2001: 148) suggests that women researching men may get a lower participation rate and by implication possibly less rich data. We disagree. This argument parallels the male role model policy prescriptions discussed in chapter 1, where the commonsense notion of match to pupils is explored. But we can no more match pupils and teachers for gender, class, race and culture than we can researchers and research participants. Such an approach guarantees neither good teaching nor research. Even if it did, gender matching has absolutely no effect on researcher power either perceived or real, in relation to participants. As Francis and Archer note (2005:93):

> respondent/researcher mismatch is not necessarily more problematic than a match, and where there is a match, there is a danger that the researcher '... may conflate experiences or distort responses in order to fit their own experiences'. (citing Reay, 1996).

Participation and data quality depend more on the nature of the research environment and the stance taken by the researchers than on their gender.

The patterns that have emerged from our engagement with the field of gender and education inform a teacher-gender time line or group life-history from past times to childhood experiences, from career choice to work experiences, from promotion to exit routes. It is this time line that underpins the structure of the book.

1
The Public Panic

A Harvard professor of psychiatry, William Pollack (cited by Phillips, 2005) has suggested that early testing of young children prejudices boys by identifying developmental delay *vis a vis* girls and that the lack of male teachers impacts most strongly on working-class boys '... where many children grow up without a father, and lack positive male role models'. But there are very many female-headed middle class families that may also lack positive male role models. Why is it that boys may be harmed by knowing they are behind girls when no one thought that girls might be harmed by boys' apparent superiority in the past? Why are boys considered more vulnerable? Is it genes, gendered psychiatry, hegemonic masculinity misogyny, patriarchy or class that Pollack is referring to? Are there causal connections for boys between missing men as fathers and teachers and their achievement, behaviour, mental wellbeing and class position, or are these really separate areas of concern that have been lumped together in both public and academic consciousness?

Introduction

Headlines such as, '*Failing boys 'public burden number one*', '*Gender gap widens to a gulf*' and '*How to improve his stories*' accompany the news that girls' exam results have not only caught up with those of boys but are also in some instances surpassing them. It seems to be quite acceptable for boys to do better than girls in education, as they have for centuries past, but not the reverse. When girls were failing, in relation to boys, there were no public calls for more female teachers as role models to help girls succeed. There was no overt concern for boys lacking male role models whist their fathers were

1

away at war many of whom were not to return. There was no panic when girls left education early, although eventually there was a policy in the second half of the twentieth century to make education more equitable for girls and boys. From the Government's perspective this was primarily to prevent wastage of economic talent and capacity rather than concern for more equal treatment. This move has clearly worked well but now we have a series of real panics on our hands about boys' underachievement relative to girls; about laddish behaviour, single parenting and female headed households, about the lack of positive male role models and a relative decline in the number of men in teaching. These many and diverse issues have coalesced around a single theme: that of missing men, particularly in education. Yet the contradictions are obvious! Men are missed when boys are deemed to suffer, be vulnerable or be unequal in relation to girls, because it goes against the natural order of things.

Are these panics justified? We think not. Instead we believe that it is important to understand the underlying features of these issues, and the expectations and processes which convert them into public panics. Is there any basis for the concerns expressed and if so what might contribute to their cause and their resolution?

In chapter 3 we map the real historical changes and developments in teaching over the past 100 years, from male teacher numbers, through boys' and girls' educational achievements in school, to the impact of teacher gender on achievement. We shall focus on the rhetoric that assumes correlation and causation.

Boys' underachievement relative to girls'

On the face of it, while both boys and girls have improved educational outcomes, girls have improved more quickly than boys and now outnumber or out-achieve boys at a variety of levels. In the white, Anglo-Saxon western world disproportionate numbers of women now go onto higher education. In the UK, for example, in 2004, 7 per cent more women than men were accepted onto undergraduate courses (UCAS figures). In the USA, where 42 per cent of undergraduates and 39 per cent of postgraduate students were women in 1970, by 2000 women constituted 56 per cent of undergraduate and 58 per cent of postgraduate students. Put another way, between 1967 and 2000 the proportion of men aged eighteen to 24 attending university in the USA declined from 33.1 to 32.6 per cent while the proportion of women doubled from 19 to 38 per cent. The change for women is quite dramatic, for men it is not and hardly warrants Phillips (2005:20) statement that 'men may be going backwards', or North's (2005:21) 'it's downhill from there'.

The main change during this period has been a focus on equal opportunity in both law and education, a widening of social and economic expectations for girls, and improved access to higher education. In addition, training for teaching and nursing, traditional female occupational destinations, moved into higher education during this period. Where girls' higher educational potential was often previously unfulfilled girls have now caught up with boys. It is hardly an excuse for public panic. Praise and congratulations might be more appropriate!

Essentially we are largely talking about white middle-class girls catching up with white middle-class boys. Getting a good career is as important as getting a husband: being a blue stocking is no longer the disadvantage it once was seen as, although residues of this can still be found (Walkerdine, 1998). The situation for working-class and ethnic minority boys and girls is different.

Gender and ethnicity

In terms of GCSE passes, higher percentages of girls than boys gain five or more passes at A* to C grades across all ethnic groups, although there are significant in-group differences. For example, 79 per cent of Chinese girls and 71 per cent of their male peers achieved this, whereas 40 per cent of Caribbean girls and 25 per cent of Caribbean boys did so (Botcherby and Hurrell, 2004:1). The percentages of ethnic minority men and women in higher education also vary (55% of men, 58% of women) but this broad category masks many variations, such as the percentage of Pakistani and Bangladeshi women being much lower than their men. This pattern is repeated in post-16 education, where only Caribbean and white women participate more than their male peers (Botcherby and Hurrell, 2004:6).

In English primary schools in 2003,

> ... in all ethnic groups, girls did better than boys in English across Key Stages 1-3, but ... results were much closer in Mathematics and Science. At age 14 the difference in the percentages of girls and boys achieving the expected level for English was in the range 12-15 percentage points for most groups. (Botcherby and Hurrell, 2004: 5)

The gender gap was highest between Caribbean girls and boys, where two-thirds of girls achieved level 5 compared to less than half of the boys.

So it is not simply a question of girls overtaking boys in terms of educational achievements but which girls, which boys and by how much. Girls who achieve and boys who do not 'do not come from the same constituency' (Reay, 2001:156). Ethnicity and class gaps are much wider than gender gaps overall and for gender the percentage differences are relatively small. Certain groups of girls, mainly middle-class girls, realise that they need educational qualifications to achieve a good career. The situation for working-class and ethnic minority girls is less clear, with marginalisation and exclusion still a strong possibility. Some groups of boys (Caribbean and white working-class) clearly have not realised this or had the opportunity to take advantage of education. However, men still get a higher proportion of first class degrees than women and still dominate academia, especially at the most senior levels. Panics about relative underachievement, if justified, must be more clearly differentiated and group-focused. As Tinklin notes (2003:323) 'Focusing on the underachievement of boys' obscures differences within genders by social class and ethnicity.' Gender alone is neither a meaningful nor helpful way to understand recent changes in relative educational underachievement. Class and ethnicity must be included too.

Boys' laddishness

Is boys' behaviour in decline? The Elton Report (1989) on discipline in schools identified problems with verbal abuse of teachers, aggression and general disruptiveness, all more associated with boys' than girls' behaviour. Boys certainly make up the majority of school exclusions, although this also varies significantly by ethnicity, with African-Caribbean boys disproportionate amongst them (Osler and Vincent, 2003:20). Aggressive and disruptive behaviour in class is much more likely to prompt exclusion and to be attributed to boys than girls by their teachers. But teachers have also been shown to have different expectations of boys and girls and of children from different ethnic groups, which may be stereotypical and discriminatory (Phoenix, 2001). However, Osler and Vincent (2003:80) argue that girls' behaviours, such as self-exclusion or self-harm,

> ... do not attract the attention of professionals, working under pressure and with a gendered view of what constitutes a behavioural problem ... (whereas) the loud and physical nature of many boys' behaviour cannot be easily ignored or overlooked.

There is a fine line to be drawn between being a lad and being disruptive or excluded from school. Research in schools repeatedly finds that some boys find it socially unacceptable to be seen to engage in academic work (Mac an Ghaill, 1994). For boys effortless achievement is often the desired image (Edwards *et al*, 1998, Power *et al*, 1998). Assertion, physicality and competitiveness are all traits of hegemonic masculinity and are for many a key feature of being a boy in school, recognised by both teachers and peer groups.

Laddish behaviour for boys is frequently defined against the feminine, as a clear marker of masculinity i.e. not what girls do. If girls read, are quiet, work hard and obey their teachers, laddish boys, by implication don't – or at least don't want to be seen to be doing so. To be real boys is to not be like girls and there is substantial peer pressure to conform to this dominant type of masculinity (Jackson, 2003). It also acts as potential cover for boys' apparent educational failure and explains their perceived lack of effort. By adopting this stance boys' laddish behaviour effectively protects them from the label of educational failure. It thus has less to do with academic ability and more to do with peer pressure to opt out and be real boys. It is a protective shield (Covington, 2000).

Willis (1977) drew a distinction between 'lads' and 'earholes' in his study of working-class boys' rejection of academic futures, effectively celebrating their disaffection from schooling. From Francis' (1998) perspective such boys may be described as 'silly and selfish', compared with girls as 'sensible and selfless' self-professed personas, but such boys are also '... often popular with children and adults ... (and) such behaviour enables individuals to present themselves as 'proper boys'' (Skelton and Francis, 2001:194-5).

What is interesting is that research from the 60s and 70s, as now, draws a clear distinction between different groups of boys. Then the focus was mainly on social class differences (Hargreaves, 1967; Lacey, 1970; Corrigan, 1979). More recently ethnic distinctions have been addressed (Gillborn and Gipps, 1996). So, is there really a significant difference in boys' and girls' school behaviours? The bad behaviour of some boys is certainly more noticeable at the moment, and widely publicised, but Osler and Vincent (2003) make a strong argument for girls' disaffection and exclusion being brought more sharply into the frame. For certain groups of girls, as well as certain groups of boys, there seem to be growing instances of disaffection and anti-social, anti-school behaviour. The point is that it makes little sense to lump all boys together. Their experiences and behaviours vary by sub-group, as will any remedies. If it is working-class laddish behaviour, adopted to define a particular style of masculinity within the peer and social group, we must understand the reasons for it so that we can address them. Some might lie within education such as the assertion of its feminisation, which we contest, but many lie within wider society and prevailing economic conditions. Whilst we all may panic about a general deterioration in standards of behaviour in society, it is not only boys, or all boys, who should be blamed.

Single parenting and female headed households

Single parenting is undoubtedly increasing. Almost one in two marriages end in divorce and it is usually fathers rather than mothers who are absent from children's lives. However, missing fathers are not a new phenomenon. Victorian fathers were not renowned for their involvement with domestic life or child rearing, and the advent of 'new men' is a relatively recent phenomenon. Fathers were also significantly absent from the hearth during periods of war yet there was no panic about boys then. Why have missing men only now been cast as detrimental to boys?

Is it because of the relatively recent focus on men in general? With the advent of second-wave feminism there has been a significant shift in the foci and theoretical underpinnings of social research. Post-modernism has brought gender issues to the fore and relegated meta-theories of class to the periphery. Men and masculinity have become the focus. Where once men, implicitly white middle class men, were the unquestioned, taken-for-granted yardstick against which women were measured, their identities, roles and behaviours have now been problematised, deconstructed and scrutinised, exposing a diverse range of subordinate and super-ordinate masculinities, to be observed, researched and explained.

In research terms we can only see things where we look. By shifting our gaze towards men and boys we see things not previously noticed: a range of identities, problems, nuances, complexities, because we are looking. As a result, men's absence from the family and from teaching is noticed, and, without substantive evidence in support, offered as the reason for boys' declining achievements in relation to girls and their so-called laddish behaviour. If male absence is the problem, the commonsense solution is to bring them back into the lives of boys, as mentors and role models, and education is an arena in which this can be planned for and managed by governments. But we need to unpick these spurious connections. Male absence is not new in families or teaching (see chapter 3), nor is poor behaviour by children, especially boys. There is a wealth of research evidence to suggest that this has been a perennial issue (Cohen, 1998). In a review of primary school behaviour Davies (1984) indicated that boys' behaviour was more problematic than girls' and that research throughout the 60s and 70s had found this to be the case. Croll and Moses (1990) make the same observation about research conducted in the 1980s: boys' behaviour in primary school was found to be worse than girls'; similarly Howe (1997), reviewing studies in the 1990s, finds that boys misbehave more than girls.

Bowlby's seminal work (1953) developed the theory of attachment. Its focus was the infant's bond with its mother, a bond he described as unique and irreplaceable. Children deprived of this early attachment lack security and consistency in their lives and can subsequently develop disturbed attachment-seeking and anti-social behaviour. Children with this primary bond are well-adjusted to the later formation of relationships with significant others, both within and outside the home, such as fathers and teachers. Later work supported Bowlby regarding attachment theory but not his stress on the unique mother-child bond. Such bonds are essential for the early development, security and well-being of the child but they can be formed with any primary carer, provided that the relationship is secure, reliable and ongoing. Contrary to Bowlby's view, mothers are no more essential to this process than are fathers. The sex of the person is irrelevant. What matters is that attachment bonds are formed early in life and maintained.

So, in single parent families, as in intact families, the key to healthy child development, male and female, is the quality of bonds made and care given. Single parent families are not ideal, nor do they necessarily have the capacity and resources to provide this kind of secure bonding and reliable care, but that is a function of economics rather than of the gender of the carer. Female headed households are no more dysfunctional for boys or girls than male headed households might be. What matters is the quality of the care within them. Bad male role models can do far more harm than male absence (Reay, 2002). There is no substantive evidence that boys are being disadvantaged by being cared for by women in the home now, with fathers absent due to divorce, or in the past with fathers absent due to different social expectations or to being away at war.

Ashley and Lee (2003) use attachment theory to differentiate parental 'caring for' children from the teachers' role of 'caring about' the children they teach and to underpin their argument that all children need and want good carers and good teachers, irrespective of their gender. Teachers are not carers in a familial Bowlbian sense. They are educators with a duty of care for their pupils which is different. It is not a permanent relationship. They cannot fulfil the attachment role, though they may be important significant others in a child's development, through 'caring about' their well-being and education. The teacher's role is distinct from that of the home or primary carer, and is concerned with widening independence and enhancing experience beyond a secure and reliable family environment.

By way of compensation for the assumed negative effect of female-headed households on boys' achievements and behaviour, male teachers as role models are proffered as the commonsense solution, despite Skelton's (2001a) finding that laddish behaviour may be partly increased through greater exposure to male teachers as boys move through the school system.

This commonsense solution is not based on sound evidence, neither does it fit with boys' views of what constitutes a good teacher, nor their own aspirations in terms of role models. Whilst politicians and parents may see it as logical and viable, children do not. For them, good teachers can be of either gender (Wragg *et al*, 2000). Ashley and Lee's boys say that they want

> ... teachers who teach well, teachers they can respect and who respect them. Teachers need to be caring but they are not expected to be substitute mothers. They are expected to keep good order, to create an environment in which learning can go on. As one boy put it 'I'd like to have a man teacher who could solve problems and that just like Mrs. B does'. (Ashley and Lee, 2003: 140)

As long ago as 1981, in the context of black under-achievement in schools, Stone (1981) argued that focusing on black role models diverted attention away from children's real needs: all children need high quality teaching by skilled teachers, regardless of race, class or gender. Matching boys to male teachers is equally a diversion from this main agenda.

Like other researchers, we have found that close bonds with parents and carers take priority when boys and girls choose role models; they are their champions and their source of inspiration, not their teachers. Beyond the family, children many choose famous personalities as role models but amongst people they know, peers are far more likely to be chosen than teachers.

Men teachers as role models for boys

There is a perception or hope that the achievements and behaviour of boys will improve if they are taught by men. This reflects essentialist notions of boys as different in terms of brain structure, educational needs and learning styles (Biddulph, 1997), that they learn and behave better when they are with men and to claims that education has become feminised. In chapter 2 we explore some of these possibilities and in chapter 3 we demonstrate that teaching has always been a predominantly female occupation, although we dispute the notion that it has recently become feminised. What we know is that many male teachers, parents, politicians and public figures see male teachers as positive role models for boys (Abbott, 2002; Phillips, 2002). The question is whether boys and girls see their teachers as role models.

We need to know why role models are considered to be so important and we must define the term role model.

Role models are considered to be crucial in the socialisation process, although they can portray a variety of stereotypical and counter-stereotypical behaviours. Where the model in question shares characteristics with the modeller, such as gender, age, race or social location, Bandura (1986) argues that the modeller is more likely to seek to emulate the model because of their shared characteristics. However, socialisation is an active process, influenced by the unique characteristics of the individual and their social context so that outcomes cannot be predetermined.

The concept of role model has a diversity of meanings attached to it through common usage and in the literature (Sargent, 2001:118). In our own research (Appendix A9; Bricheno and Thornton, 2005) we took a dictionary definition of role model, namely a person you respect, follow, look up to or want to be like. The definition used by Vescio *et al* (2004:2) is very similar, that is someone 'to imitate, to be like', and 'perceived as exemplary and worthy'.

We asked primary and secondary pupils to choose attributes of a role model, to identify their most important role model, to say which attributes were most important to them and to write about their own role models.

What did we find?

Neither boys nor girls in this study saw their teachers as role models. As in many similar surveys (Carrington and Skelton, 2003; *Education News*, 2000; *Junior Achievement*, 2003; Vescio *et al*, 2004), parents and close relatives were the most frequently chosen role models for boys and girls. This supports attachment theory principles of close bonds with carers who are seen as reliable, constant champions who children most want to emulate. We found that boys were less likely than girls to have any role models at all (64 per cent and 76 per cent respectively).

The most important attributes for a role model were caring and trust, attributes often associated with parents and carers but less frequently with teachers. Typical examples of both boys and girls naming caring attributes include:

> *Kind, loving, helpful* (girl, aged 10)
>
> *Doesn't lie, being able to listen to what other people have to say, be kind always* (girl, aged 11)
>
> *I think a role model is a good kind person who helps people when they are in need* (boy, aged 12)
>
> *Nice and understanding and when you are upset they look out for you* (boy, aged 14).

There were some important gender differences, with far more girls selecting caring, kindness and trust as the most important attribute whilst boys were more likely than girls to select surface attributes such as looks, fame, success and money. However, whilst there are big differences between boys and girls for caring and kind they all clearly said that this was the most important attribute for a role model.

Who are their role models?

Relatives were the most important role models for boys and girls. For girls friends came second and for boys it was footballers. Pop stars were third in popularity for girls but only sixth for boys. Very few teachers were named; they came sixth for girls and ninth for boys (see Table 1).

Friends, although of less importance to boys than footballers, were mentioned more frequently than were teachers, supporting the findings of many others (Ashley and Lee, 2003; Williams, 1980) who have indicated that peers are much more important to both boys and girls in identity construction than are their teachers. Only 2.4 per cent of pupils in our study referred to teachers as role models compared with 9.8 per cent who referred to peers.

Parents and relatives are by far the most popular role models, girls more frequently choosing female relatives and boys choosing male relatives (see Figure 1).

Table 1: Most important role models for boys and girls ranked by popularity

Role models	Girls Rank	n	Role models	Boys Rank	n
Relatives	1	98	Relatives	1	65
Friends	2	15	Footballer	2	24
Pop music	3	11	Friends	3	6
Film or TV	4	6	Other	4	6
Footballer	5	3	Other sport	5	6
teachers	6	3	Pop music	6	4
Famous	7	3	fictional	7	5
Caring professions	8	2	Film or TV	8	3
Other	9	1	teachers	9	2
Music and arts	10	1	Famous	10	2
fictional	11	1	Comedian	11	2
Total named		144	Total named		125

Figure 1: Relatives as role models by sex (responses to Q6)

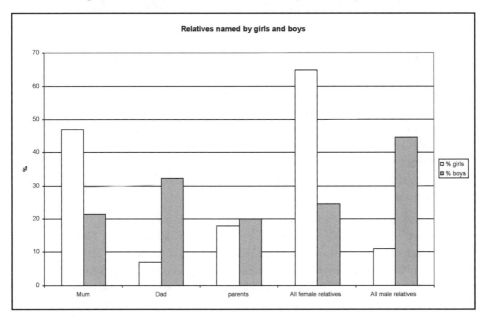

A similar pattern emerged when we looked at role models outside the family. Boys had a very small number of female role models, and these were almost exclusively relatives, whereas girls named male role models in the majority of categories (see Table 1).

Thirty boys cited sportsmen as their most important role model, 24 of whom were footballers. Beckham, England's Captain, was the most frequently named male non-relative role model for boys alongside a wide range of other famous sportsmen, mostly footballers.

Footballers came close to fathers as the most important role models for boys. David Beckham was described as caring, kind and charitable, as well as a gifted footballer, by three boys, as was the caring role model assigned to relatives.

Q.6. David Beckham

Q.7. I have always loved sports, especially football. I feel David is a person with a special gift, he has stuck with this sport (and team), through good times and bad. He always gives 110 per cent in everything he does, and he's very caring and kind. He auctions some of his most prized possessions to charity and spends thousands of pounds on charity parties at his house. Overall, he has most of the qualities I think someone needs to be a role model. (Boy, aged 16)

However, the descriptions of other footballers were limited primarily to sporting skills and team affiliation, which suggests a hero type of role model, representing stereotypical masculine traits. Boys' choice of sporting heroes can thus be seen as reinforcing their masculinity along hegemonic lines.

The prominence of footballers as role models for boys might be the result of media coverage. Television offers boys and girls images, models and fantasies of what it is to be a proper man or woman. The British Government is actively promoting the use of footballers as role models: 'Playing for success' (Department for Education and Skills (DfES) 1997), the government's after-school scheme, promotes professional footballers as role models and the National Reading Campaign (2003) uses football heroes to encourage boys, and apparently girls also, to read.

Motivating boys to read has hit the headlines following growing evidence that, overall, boys are falling behind girls in achievement. This has led many schools to look for role models to encourage boys (and girls) to read. What better place to start than with local sporting heroes? As the UK's most popular sport, much of this activity is focused on football. (NLT, 2003).

Equally the Football League's Head of Education, Kate Coleman, suggests 'It is all about using the power of football to inspire and motivate children who may need a bit of a push' (Paton and Lee, 2005:6).

However, Connell (1982) views school sport as a heavily gendered masculinising process and suggests that football can be used as a means of actively reinforcing a masculine stereotype. For this reason, Skelton (2001b) is critical of the government's scheme which promotes professional footballers as role models. However, many schools, recognising children's attraction to famous personalities, are developing a visits programme which makes use of sports personalities to promote certain qualities such as courage, patience, maturity, dedication, through talks and discussions with students. Ashley and Lee (2003) would prefer to see the range of boys' interests extended into more artistic fields, rather than limiting them to stereotypical areas of interest.

There is clearly a contradiction here. Footballers are seen as role models for boys and by boys, yet '... undesirable behaviour on their part can set an unfortunate example' (Lord Woolf, cited by Cohen, 2005: 31).

Several famous footballers have been in trouble for swearing and violence on and off the pitch (Paton and Lee, 2005:6) and it is not surprising that some educators are now describing them as 'a bad example to British youth' (Aaronovitch, 2005:29). This is hardly the stuff of positive role models but the point is that some are good and some less so.

> Rooney doesn't seem to be cast in the mould of the super cool teen-age stars such as Bjorn Borg and Boris Becker, who planned their careers brilliantly and with middle-aged caution. David Beckham, for all the jokes, has managed his life with enormous skill. Rooney seems to be a teenager like I was a teenager – silly, careless and (talent apart) ordinary. (Aaronovitch, 2005:29).

Beckham's life-style and image have been the subject of academic study and it is thought that he presents a 'new man' public image to boys who wish to emulate their sporting heroes. Although two girls named footballers as male role models, none named Beckham. This could be seen as surprising given his wife's high profile in the entertainment world and girls' apparent interest in attributes such as good looks and girl singers.

The descriptions of other footballers are limited primarily to sporting skills and team affiliation. The latter is the more common heroic macho description given by these boys of footballers as role models and better fits the traits of hegemonic masculinity than the stereotypical mix of male and female traits assigned to Beckham.

Q.6. Denis Bergkamp

Q.7. Because he's the best person on Arsenal (Boy, aged 10)

Q.6. Robbie Keane

Q.7. Because he scores a lot of goals for Tottenham (Boy, aged 16)

Boys were more likely to name a footballer (24) than their father (21) as their most important role model.

Table 2: Boys: All Role Models and Most Important Role Model

Role models	Boys Q5 All role models	Boys Q6 Most important role model
Film or TV	13	3
Footballer	57	24
Pop music	14	5
Other sport	9	6
Dad	39	21

Teachers as role models

Only nine references in total (out of 269) were made to teachers, and just three girls and two boys named their teacher as their most important role model.

My father, my cello teacher, my godmother (Girl, aged 14)

Parents and teachers (Boy, aged 14)

Close friends or relatives are highly likely to share some characteristics with the children who choose them as role models, such as gender, social location or race. In Bandura's (1986) terms, they share model-observer similarity, and in the theory of social learning, it should not be surprising that children seek to emulate those who are similar to themselves in some significant ways.

That only 2.4 per cent of all pupils referred to a teacher as a role model strongly suggests that children do not see their teachers as role models. Maybe these pupils respect or look up to their teachers but, when thinking about role models, also focus on things such as 'want to be like' and 'follow'. If so, this might indicate a lack of desire to become like their teachers.

Our sample clearly favoured role models from their direct social environment such as friends or relatives but there is no indication that these boys or girls identify with their teachers, male or female. They do not see their teachers as role models. As a policy prescription to remedy boys' so-called underachievement and laddish behaviour it simply isn't working.

However, the promotion of footballers as role models for boys may be having some degree of success, perhaps because it attaches literacy to an already popular and successful image rather than seeking to create a new image – that of male teachers who do not have the powerful masculine accoutrements of fame, physical prowess, money that attracts some boys to footballers as role models.

Looking back later in life

There are some clear differences between children's and adults' views about role models. The *TES* series, 'My best teacher' clearly shows that many adults, looking back, identify some of their teachers as inspirational role models and there is ample evidence that many parents would like their sons to see their male teachers as role models, especially single mothers of young boys (Sargent, 2001). When 1,000 adults were asked to name the best role models for children in a recent UK poll (Cooperative Insurance Society, 2001) 79 per cent chose teachers. But all this comes with hindsight, greater experience and from an adult perspective. If children are asked, teachers are generally not chosen (Bromnick and Swallow, 1999; Biskup, and Pfister, 1999; HON News, 2003).

Conclusions

The education-based male role models that are available to children clearly illustrate that men continue to hold high status positions such as headships, that they predominantly assume responsibility for high status subjects such as Maths and Science and that they receive extra pay for doing so (Alexander 1991, chapter 7). Almost exclusively they teach in the higher status age-ranges such as older children and juniors but preferably years 5 and 6. It could therefore be argued that primary children not only require more male role models, evenly and proportionately distributed across all primary teaching jobs and positions, but also more powerful female role models in senior, high status positions.

Whilst evidence exists that undermines public panics about boys' achievements, laddish behaviour and missing men, it is rarely acknowledged beyond academia. Government ministers and their shadow counterparts continue to encourage 'men to work as childminders – providing in the process, male role models for single parent families headed by women' (Margaret Hodge cited by Hill, 2005:7), to 'identify the barriers to boys' learning... and ensure that there are more good male role models to challenge boys' resistance to learning (and their laddish behaviour)' (David Blunkett, DfES, 2000), and to call for boys to be taught in single-sex schools with strong male role models to help a 'lost generation' of fatherless young men find their way in life'(Liam Fox, cited Hinsliff and Tenko 2005:13). Even the educational press, which should know better, plays a part in perpetuating the panics, frequently headlining 'problems with boys' and even claiming that the dearth of men teachers, and thus the education of children by women 'damages children's education, equal opportunities, and society in general' (*Opinion*, 2002:22).

In this chapter we have looked at the panics and the simplistic but unproven solutions prescribed. In chapter 2 we look at the theories which support and undermine them.

Recommended reading

Caroline Jackson's exploration of laddishness in schools clarifies many of the ways in which boys construct their masculinity in opposition to things feminine, and Chris Skelton and Bruce Carrington's work on unpicking the concept of role models is well worth reading.

Jackson, C. (2003) Motives for 'Laddishness' at School: fear of failure and fear of the feminine, *British Journal of Educational Research*, 29 (4) p583-598.

Carrington, B., and Skelton, C., (2003) Re-thinking 'role models': equal opportunities in teacher recruitment in England and Wales, in *Journal of Education Policy*, 18 (3): 253-265.

2
Explanations of Gender Differences

Introduction

I s it about sex or gender? About genetic endowment or social conditioning? Are sex traits natural? Are men and women separate homogeneous groups? Our sex is determined in the womb. Biologically we are either men or women (with but a few rare exceptions). Does gender follow automatically from sex? Is it in our genes to behave in specifically male and female ways? We need to consider what role, if any, biological sex, gendered social experience and human agency play in the formation of our gender identities.

Is it in the genes?

There is a resurgence of work on the influence genes might have on human behaviour and learning although there remain few conclusive studies of their impact. The thorny issue of genetic influence on intelligence has been around a long time but despite recent advances in the science of genetics even this has yet to be fully determined. While the IQs of children are generally found to be similar to their parents, twin studies involving adoptees suggest IQ scores can vary significantly between adopted children and their biological parents, especially if adoption takes place at an early age (Van Ijzendoorn *et al*, 2005). When later adoption takes place greater similarity of IQ between adopted children and their biological parents is found. This suggests child-rearing practices and early experiences in the home have a strong influence on IQ outcomes and it certainly isn't all in the genes!

Baron-Cohen (2003) argues that male and female brains are different, not just in size (men's are larger) but, more importantly in terms of their wiring. He defines the standard male brain as 'S' type, meaning systemising, hard-wired to understand and build systems and the standard female brain as 'E' type, empathetic, hard-wired to be sensitive to and empathise with people and strong on communication. These different brain types are thought to be due to genetic differences honed through human evolution. Baron-Cohen evidences them through his study of people with autism, three-quarters of whom are male, and all of whom, by definition (Frith, 1989), have a triad of difficulties that include poor communication, little imagination and lacking social skills such as empathy, but sometimes also having exceptional abilities in understanding complex mechanical or artistic systems. In autism he claims to have found an extreme version of the male brain.

Baron-Cohen's thesis fits with Moir and Moir's (1998) view that boys are genetically different from girls, that they are programmed differently and that this should be recognised in terms of their treatment within education. It also fits with sex role theory which suggests that women *nest* to protect and nurture the family, that they are the world's communicators and carers, whilst men plan, organise, make and control things to assert their independence, protect themselves and promulgate their genes. All are fundamentally essentialist views of gendered behaviour. If the biology of the brain makes us like this then it would potentially explain why there are gender-segregated roles and occupations, including teaching, why girls as babies are more socially interactive, pay greater attention to faces and speak, read and write earlier than boys, why boys play with mechanical objects, build things and have enhanced spatial abilities, why there are more male than female scientists and mathematicians, and why, according to the President of Harvard, Larry Summers, there are so few senior women in Science and Mathematics departments at top universities.

Summers' view is supported by Dr Sandra Witelson, a neurosurgeon, who suggests that boys and girls react to the world in different ways, because they have different levels of sex hormones (testosterone, and oestrogen), which results in men being better able to separate cognitive and emotional issues. This, she argues, can lead to women being disadvantaged, particularly when undertaking important, stressful jobs (cited McKie and Harris, 2005:18). Summers' view is also supported by Dr Helena Cronin (2005), an evolutionary scientist, who argues

> ... that there are, on average, sex differences in dispositions, interests and values. Men are far more competitive, ambitious, status-conscious and single-minded: and they'd rather work with abstract ideas or objects than with humans. Women are more focused on family and other relationships; they have wider interests and prefer not to work in people-free zones. (p21)

As a Darwinian, Cronin suggests these differences arise from the evolution of the human species over time and are consistent across cultures and throughout history. However, a geneticist (Jones, 2003) claims that, 'the idea that differences in brain-wiring account for the lack of senior female academics in science is untenable'. He gives the following example:

> There are very few Jews in farming but that doesn't mean they cannot farm. It is all to do with background, and until you can eliminate the issue, you cannot make the generalisations Summers has made. (cited McKie and Harris, 2005:18)

Geake (2005) argues that as human beings are biological entities, their behaviour is also biologically influenced. He is concerned that educationalists engage in dialogue with cognitive neuroscientists since they might usefully contribute to our understanding of learning and behaviour. Whilst what we learn is not predetermined, our propensity to learn is biologically influenced. He cites the neuronal plasticity of infants' brains as one reason why most young children acquire their first language with ease yet struggle in later years to learn a second language and why it is more difficult for adults to learn new things. This explanation supports the adopted twin study finding of early childhood experiences having lasting impact on later IQ. Neuroscience may therefore identify what the best age for early education might be. Neuroscience also suggests that

> Concepts learned in childhood can be very resilient to change later in school e.g. naïve science. In sum, what the brain has reinforced stays that way, only its salience attenuating with non-use. (Geake, 2005:11)

Neuroscience also informs our understanding of some learning difficulties, such as dyslexia and ADHD. In the future it may also be able to say something helpful regarding why boys and girls appear to think differently and achieve differently in school. However, it is not an exact science and many of its theories rest on data obtained from laboratory experiments. Over-simplification of complex findings from laboratory experiments in terms of school practises can lead to what Geake terms *neuro-nonsense*. He cites DfES endorsement of the use of pupil learning styles in schools as one such example which over-simplifies something which is highly complex.

Hines (cited Rutter 2004:24-25) identifies, from a psychological perspective, the considerable overlap between men and women when psychological traits are studied and notes that there is more variation within groups of men and groups of women than there is between men and women. This is in accord with our position. We recognise much gender diversity within male and female populations and reject any notion that the behaviour of either men or women is entirely pre-determined by their genes. Some conform to stereotypical sex roles, others do not. There is more social variety than genetic or evolutionary theories would suggest and more opportunity to change according to our lived experiences. Biological, sex-based predispositions may evolve and change over time but not within this book's time scales. There have been significant changes in relative boys' and girls' educational achievements over the past 50 years and in male and female life-styles and social roles which have happened far too rapidly to be explained by evolutionary biology!

Sex or gender: innate or learned behaviour?

Our sex is determined by our genes and physiology. Biologically we are usually either male or female whereas gender is socially constructed around our biological sex. It is formed from our experiences and interactions in a social world, which varies in time and location. So it is only possible to understand specific gender identities through reference to the culture of the society from which they arise and the historical period in which they are located. Whereas there are two biological sexes, male and female, there are multiple variations in gender identities. From a situation of being either masculine or feminine there is a continuum of masculinities and femininities at the extremes of which lie hegemonic masculinity and stereotypical femininity. Kohlberg (1966) suggests that the gender identity we acquire is a combination of social learning, mediated by maturational and cognitive factors and that as we grow and experience new things we actively organise our own identities: we have choice and agency. Nevertheless, there is a strong element of social conditioning in the growth of gender identities.

Our experiences and the nature of our interactions are strongly influenced by our biological sex because people in our social networks frequently respond to us in sex-specific stereotypical ways. Despite this, there is far more scope for individual and group variation in our gender identities than in our sexual identities. We may be gay or heterosexual men or women but the possible variations on masculinity and femininity are infinite. Being deemed feminine or masculine was different in Victorian times from what it is in 21st century Britain and it varies now across different cultures, races, classes and religions. Unlike our biological sex, our gender identities are not fixed at birth, they are acquired through social interaction. Sex and gender are not synonymous (Cheng, 1996). Our genetic inheritance may predispose us to certain traits and behaviours; these may be reinforced by our life experiences and others expectations of us but we are not determined by them. What we can learn from biology and neuroscience is that our early learning may be more difficult to change in later life.

Our perspective hinges upon the social construction of identity differences, and this changes over time. If genetic endowment *causes* boys to be better at Science, for example, why has the gender gap in Science examinations narrowed so dramatically in the past 30 years (Arnot and Phipps, 2003)? Women in the 1970s achieved one in ten Science and Engineering PhDs. Now they get one in three in Science (McKie and Harris, 2005:18). If genetic endowment 'causes' women to be home-makers why are so many women now in paid work compared with 30 years ago (Bower, 2001)? In evolutionary terms such changes have been far too sudden for biological explanations to be viable. Explanations must therefore be socially and historically located: identifiable patterns within gender identities and roles, however temporal and transitory, are seen to result from social rather than normative or biological forces (Paechter, 1998).

What has happened within social structures and social processes that has caused such relatively rapid change in gendered outcomes and behaviour?

Social explanations

Although it is well established that boys are more prone to 'genetic disorders, early illness and accidents', and that this may explain their disproportionate representation within the category of Special Educational Needs, Riddell *et al* (2001:94) argue that culture and socialisation also have a strong influence on how those needs are experienced and treated. People generally respond differently to boys and girls with Special Educational Needs (SEN) in much the same way as they respond differently to babies according to their sex. Boys are seen as strong, and handsome: girls as sweet and pretty. Boys are told not to cry: girls to share and care for others. Differential perceptions, responses and treatment, from the moment of birth, help to socialise us all into gendered men and women. Relatives and friends may offer sex-appropriate toys (Smith and Lloyd, 1978) and sex-appropriate life experiences, which serve to shape and reinforce our gendered experiences and expectations.

Our gendered socialisation is well advanced by the time we reach school but it continues there as well. Teachers' expectations of pupils often show clear gender patterns. For example, men and women teachers have been found to have different expectations of behaviour for boys and girls (Eccles *et al*, 1993). They also have different expectations of ability. Goldberg (1968) found that affixing male or female names to essays led to different marks: those assigned a male name were marked higher. This is partly why formal examination scripts are now marked anonymously. Walkerdine (1998) found that teachers praised girls for working hard and boys for being clever. In a similar vein, Murphy and Elwood's (1998) teachers saw girls' as achievements to be the result of diligence but boys' as the result of natural ability; boys' failures were explained by their lack of effort, whereas girls' failures were seen as due to lack of ability. When boys do better than girls, especially at the highest levels, such as the Advanced Extension Awards at 'A' level, it is seen as confirmation that they really are more clever and as an explanation for why we still have the glass ceiling (Smithers, cited Henry, 2002). However, Weinberg (1979) found that sex differences disappeared on a physical endurance task if female subjects were given raised expectations and male subjects' expectations were lowered, which suggests that where differences are observed, they are the result of differential expectations based on prior gendered socialisation.

Schools have an important strategic influence on the development of masculine and feminine identities but, as Connell argues (1989), the family, the work place and sexual relations have a more potent influence. Our gendered identities are formed in social contexts, not in a vacuum.

> ... the strongest effects of schooling on the construction of masculinity are the indirect effects of streaming and failure, authority pattern, the academic curriculum and definitions of knowledge – rather than the direct effects of equity programmes on courses dealing with gender. (Connell, 1989:291)

The social contexts in which our gender identities form are intersected by class, culture and race so while it is perfectly possible to say that men are more likely than women to cheat in their studies, we can also say that those with lower intelligence are more likely to cheat (both men and women), and that less intelligent men are more likely to cheat than men with high intelligence (Szabo and Underwood, 2004:185). Not all men are the same, simply because they are men!

Nevertheless, the characteristics normally associated with stereo-typical male behaviour (hegemonic masculinity) include com-petitiveness that can lead to aggression, displays of physical strength, concealment of feelings, rationality and independence, as well as

> ... restrictive emotionality, concern with power and status, excessive self-reliance, homophobia, anti-authoritarian bravado, anti-intellec-tualism and non-relational attitudes to sexuality (which) are quite dysfunctional for many males. (Bonner, 1997:3-4)

Pro-feminists in the men's movement recognise a tendency within patriarchal systems such as ours for men to suppress or keep hidden any self-doubts they have about making the masculine grade (Kauf-man, 1994). The suggestion is that to express such doubts makes them feel powerless, and vulnerable to accusations of not being *real* men. In this context it is not surprising that Askew and Ross (1988) describe power play as underlying many male interactions, with a constant jockeying for positions that carry high status and prestige. This is demonstrated in the educational literature that depicts hyper-confident boys and men working alongside hyper-competent girls and women in our schools. Men tend to overstate their com-petence (Flintoff, 1993: 82), women to understate it (Wilder and Powell, 1989; Cubillo, 1999). Boys have more positive beliefs than girls about their competence in Sport and Maths, although girls are more positive about English (Eccles *et al* 1993; Fredricks and Eccles, 2002). Ryan and Pintrich (1997) suggest that girls feel more cog-nitively competent than boys but boys rarely express doubts about their abilities. Davies *et al* (2005), confirm this, finding that boys are more likely to be bold and adaptable in their learning, 'more reckless or overconfident' (p31) able to 'respond to uncertainty more decisively' (p36), and more likely to think they know the answer to a problem (p38).

This self-confidence and a propensity for guessing can lead to boys getting more answers right than girls, who are stereotypically more indecisive, but also get more answers wrong. The spread of boys'

educational achievements tends to be much wider, from excep-
tionally able to having no qualifications at all (Cronin, 2005). This
drive for high status makes boys and men generally more goal-
oriented, seeking extrinsic status and reward, whereas girls and
women seem to be more task-oriented, and intrinsically motivated
(Dweck *et al*, 1978). Stereotypically, women as leaders tend to be
facilitators, people-oriented and team managers whereas men as
leaders tend to be directors, task-oriented with more *laissez-faire*
attitudes (Davidson and Ferrario, 1992).

All this may have its roots in biological predispositions but ultimately this is socially adapted behaviour. It varies between boys and
men and it can change. Where such behaviours occur there are likely
to be underlying social motivations. For instance, for many boys in
school, higher status amongst their peers comes from giving the
appearance of effortless learning (Osler and Vincent, 2003), leading
them to deny that they have worked hard even when they have. In
this high stakes status game failure is better attributed to lack of
interest, concern or hard work than to any lack of competence or
ability because that would lower their standing within the peer
group. Gender identity is therefore a social not a biological construct
(Connell, 1995; Barret 2001; Woodward 1998).

By way of contrast there is a notion in the literature that men are
more vulnerable, weaker than women in their biological, psychological and social make-up. The position of men in society has
changed. Where misogyny, patriarchy and homophobia were once
hidden, taken for granted, they are now, thanks to feminism and
legislative changes, exposed, debated and challenged in the public
arena. Perceptions of men and masculinity are changing and gender
identity is much more of an issue. The behaviour of men and boys is
publicly scrutinised and frequently derided. Such public exposure
adds to their vulnerability. The negative threads of hegemonic masculinity (anti-academic laddish behaviour, competitiveness, aggression, abuse and violence) stand in contradiction to the *new* man
version of masculinity (fashion conscious, emotionally literate, caring and nurturing), posited by some as the positive new male role
models for the next generation of boys. Yet, in teaching, it is the
hegemonic version of masculinity that is sought by female single
parents and sometimes by appointment panels. Men are missing
from education but what kind of men are wanted? What role are they
to play?

The field of education

Bourdieu's theory of cultural and social capital helps us

> ...account for the interplay between structural conditions, individual agency and identity and its effects on dispositions and activities within educational programs and career-decision making. (Grenfell and Jones, 1998, cited Ecclestone and Pryer, 2003: 474).

In the field of education there is a continuing power struggle over who commands the resources, the curriculum, the ethos and intended outcomes of education. It may be politicians or economists, government or governors, pupils or parents, teachers or head-teachers, or male or female teachers. And it varies by level. In the classroom, and in much of initial teacher education, women outnumber men. At the upper levels the reverse is true. During much of the 20th century, as we shall see in chapter 3, the curriculum, ethos and outcomes of education (particularly but not only in primary schools) were often more closely aligned with stereotypical female dispositions and traits, such as care, nurture and child-centredness.

One strategy to gain power in the educational field is to promote a particular curriculum or pedagogy as imparting the most legitimate way forward. This might be seen as applying to the Education Reform Act (ERA, Department of Education and Science (DES) 1989), which fundamentally changed the way in which the curriculum was structured and assessed in England and Wales and which subsequently led to prescriptive pedagogies and a realignment of control, away from teachers (predominantly female) and head-teachers into the hands of governments, politicians and their innumerable quangos.

According to Bourdieu and Passeron (1977), depending on their position within the field, different people will develop different sets of dispositions, inclinations or attitudes which inform their actions. The dispositions pupils and teachers are exposed to, and thus encouraged to develop, will vary according to which school they attend or teach in and its place in the educational field. These dispositions will have gendered aspects to them although they are ultimately determined neither by our genes nor the social structures and processes which shape them. Rather, they are the outcome of a complex mixing of individual agency and socialisation, what Berger (1963) termed, Man in Society – Society in Man and what Bourdieu terms *habitus*. Habitus is acquired in the family. It underlines all the child's experiences in the wider world but it is also changed by those experiences (Ecclestone and Pryor, 2003).

The part played by gender may be more evident in some fields than others. For example, within military cultures, the rituals, norms, values and structures reflect distinctive conceptions of men and women. Klein (1999:47) holds that,

> ... military service can be described as a rite of passage to male adulthood, teaching toughness, and trying to eliminate what is regarded to be effeminate. These gendered identities are by no means monolithic – there are different forms of masculinity and different relationships between them.

However, male-dominated fields serve as important spaces for the reinforcement of hegemonic masculinity. The military may be an extreme context, but Flintoff (1993) notes something similar occurring in the training of Physical Education teachers at Brickhill College. Here hegemonic masculinity was built around male hyper-confidence in themselves and their abilities and the verbal put-down of women peers and non-hegemonic males.

Although the social construction of gendered identities in education is generally thought to be weaker and less overt than in military fields, cumulative research suggests that patterns can be identified. Our personal characteristics and identity prior to entering education, plus our experiences of education, have significant implications for the forms of masculinity and femininity we adopt as pupils and students and subsequently as teachers.

Centrality and integration: must men be central?

Much academic research on student drop-out in the past 25 years has focused on the model developed in the mid-1970s by Vincent Tinto, who theorised that a major influence on student decisions to persist or drop out of college is their ability to integrate into both the social and academic worlds in which they find themselves. Each university or college department has its own prevailing ethos and values at its centre, a dominant sub-culture, which defines the standards of judgement for all its members.

> The periphery, in turn, comprises other communities or subcultures whose particular values, beliefs, and patterns of behaviour may differ substantially from those of the centre. (Tinto, 1993:60).

The Tinto model suggests that members of educational communities who are centrally located, who are in tune with the dominant sub-culture, are more likely to see themselves as fitting in, are more committed and less likely to withdraw or leave. Thus, the success of students may, 'hinge upon their centrality to institutional life' (Tinto, 1993:62). A number of variables, such as race, secondary academic performance, parental encouragement and gender interact to form students' initial commitment to the college campus and to educational goals. These initial commitments are modified over time as students integrate into the campus community. Tinto theorises that successful integration enhances these commitments and positively influences students' intentions to persist.

Centrality, commitment and integration are important concepts in relation to men in teaching. In chapter 4 there is substantial empirical evidence that for many, if not most men, teaching is not their first choice of career and, in chapter 6, that in the predominantly female training and work environment of primary education men find it difficult to complete their training successfully and to integrate well with their mainly female student and qualified teacher peers.

While Tinto's model can be criticised for making assumptions about how students reach drop-out decisions without taking their views and feelings into consideration, more recent research focuses on the social processes affecting students' decisions. Following Tinto, Thomas (2000) suggests that social network analysis may provide a unique way of understanding social integration and his study indicates that centrality has a small but direct impact on student persistence.

> Centrality can be broadly conceptualised as the degree to which the network or an individual in the network is in a position to influence others in the group or network ... It is often assumed that persons at the centre of the network, on whom many others are dependent, are in more central, and hence more powerful, positions than those located on the periphery of the group. (Thomas, 2000: 596)

In the field of teaching and teacher education women are currently more likely to occupy this central position and have a greater impact on its defining ethos and values, at least at the entry levels of training and employment, where they far outnumber men. Men here are de-centred, on the periphery in terms of sub-culture, integration and, most importantly, power. A similar situation might be expected to apply where small numbers of women enrol in predominantly male courses such as Engineering (see chapter 6).

Centrality is directly linked to power. Men are generally perceived to occupy more powerful positions in society than women. Certain expectations accompany this positioning, in terms of impact and voice. Men generally occupy central positions, women are on the periphery. As Kimmel (1994:125) notes that 'the hegemonic definition of manhood is a man in power, a man with power and a man of power'.

This is not the case in the education world though, especially in primary education. Here the reverse may be true, particularly at the level at which male students and newly-qualified male entrants to the teaching profession engage with education. For men on an Education campus, there are difficulties in establishing an extensive social network: there are few men on the same course, the nature of the Education course means that little time is available for extending social networks beyond student peers. Once on a teaching placement, social networks and personal influence are reduced even further: the student's role is not an influential one and the staffroom is inhabited predominantly by women teachers. In these contexts men generally are not in power. They are de-centred, stripped of societal and personal expectations of power which have been conferred on them by hegemonic notions of masculinity.

In teacher training, especially primary teaching, power is differently located: women and men, as individuals and as groups, are differently positioned within the power frameworks that operate. Unlike in other social contexts, women are more likely to occupy dominant professional status. Men entering teaching are expected to adopt a non-hegemonic, subordinate version of masculinity.

Paechter (1998) argues that subordinate men may still be dominant *vis-à-vis* women as are male primary headteachers and heads of teacher training but at the recruitment, selection, student and newly qualified stages of their careers men are not likely to be dominant. At this point theories of integration, processes of decision-making and the concept of centrality are important because they help explain how men, as individuals and as a group, experience social discontinuity and loss of influence over women: they are not central to the professional or student peer group culture, others are not dependent on them, they are located on the periphery and they lack power. When this happens it may well exacerbate other factors which have been associated with male absence from education in general and from teacher training courses in particular. Lack of commitment, such as not pro-actively choosing primary teaching as a career (Ozga and Sukhnandan, 1998), lack of supportive peer networks, lack of a male ethos, lack of centrality and of power, may exacerbate male drop-out rates in training and during the early stages of a teaching career. The power and status expectations of men entering predominantly female education fields may be unrealistic and unmet, at least in the early stages of their career (Reid and Thornton, 2000).

When men do enter teaching, especially primary teaching, much of what is familiar may be removed and replaced with something that is probably unfamiliar and uncertain. Like other minorities, '...they are likely to experience a sense of isolation and/or incongruence' (Tinto, 1993: 74). They may feel alienated (Case, 2005). In this setting it is far more difficult for men to subordinate and marginalise women, although it is recognised that such actions operate along a continuum: as the age of pupils taught rises and levels of seniority increase so does the presence of men and thus their power in the education field. The concepts of centrality and social integration help to explain both the lack of men in teaching and their experiences when they seek to enter this predominantly female occupation.

Re-centring and Re-integration

Zepke and Leach (2005:50) use Tinto's theory of integration to explore a number of studies related to student retention and marginalised groups. They found in a large number of studies that student outcomes were improved if

- personal contact outside classrooms was promoted

- a commitment was made to students' total well-being, for example by facilitating social networks

- students were 'involved in some kind of academic learning community... (for example), homogenous groups based on a shared ethnic, gender or religious ethos.'

- social isolation, feelings of alienation and difficulty making friends was addressed.

In other words, those on the periphery, whoever they are, need to be re-centred, re-integrated and supported. One mechanism might be to enhance student peer support structures (see Appendix A4, the Men's Club). For the minority, in this case men, this will be difficult because of low numbers. Alternatively, they might be supported in activating female peer support and friendship networks, based on commonality of professional commitments to teaching, to improve outcomes. For men as a group this will involve a big shift from a socialised expectation of dominance to immersion in a predominantly female world in which they don't readily fit as a group, although as individuals many do.

Citing Tierney (2000:219), Zepke and Leach argue that integration can also be achieved through forms of institutional adaptation.

> Rather than a model that assumes that students must fit into what is often an alien culture and that they leave their own cultures, I argue the opposite. The challenge is to develop ways in which an individual's identity is affirmed, honoured and incorporated into the organisation's culture. (Zepke and Leach, 2005:52)

This is a familiar argument in terms of integrating minority and under-represented groups into higher education. Rather than making the students fit the organisation better, the challenge is to change the organisation and its values to fit an increasingly diverse student population better. Different motivations, values, beliefs and interactive styles should be recognised and accepted as equally valuable. However, even when they are located on large diverse campuses, education departments in the UK are largely self-contained and inward looking. Class commitments, placements and term dates extend well beyond those of other departments and disciplines, apart from nursing, and they are ruled more by government quangos and inspection regimes than by university systems. So, the opportunity to '...provide a greater array of niches into which a wider range of persons may find their place', (Tinto, 1993:124) is limited.

In chapter 3 we map the changes that have taken place over the past 100 years in male/female teacher numbers and boys' and girls' achievements, demonstrating that whilst some things have changed significantly, others remain largely the same. One significant but largely un-remarked change has been in the structure and ethos of education, its pedagogies, curriculum and assessment. Following the ERA (DES, 1989), and confirming that familiar patterns and dispositions do change over time, education has become increasingly masculine in orientation, in terms of its formal structures, central control over the curriculum and pedagogy, subject specialisms and hierarchies (Thornton, 1998), competitive assessments and league-table rankings (Mahony and Hextall, 2000). To use Baron-Cohen's terms, education and teaching has become more systemised, creating a better alignment with what he describes as the male brain, and what we might understand better as socially reinforced and enacted genetic predispositions. As this structural variation permeates down through education levels it may well make teaching, particularly primary teaching, a more attractive occupation for men to enter and feel comfortable in. Rather than change men to fit in to the field of education through assimilation into a predominantly female domain and their adoption of *new* men subordinate masculinities, the education system is changing to fit hegemonic male predispositions better. Perhaps, in time, education will become a field in which men are central and women are de-centred. The pendulum is certainly swinging in that direction!

Recommended reading

Moir, A. and Moir, B. (1998) *Why Men Don't Iron: The Real Science of Gender Studies*, London: Harper Collins, present a case for the biological basis of gender differences.

Jones, S. (2003) *The Descent of Men*, Boston: Houghton Mifflin, provides a more balanced view in terms of nature/nurture disputes.

3
Myths and Reality

Introduction

Currently, 93 per cent of educational assistants, 72 per cent of education sector employees and 54 per cent of secondary school teachers are women; 31 per cent of secondary school heads, 27 per cent of further education college principles and 15 per cent of university vice-chancellors are women (EOC, 2005). Clearly women outnumber men in education at the chalk face, but not when it comes to educational leadership at post-primary school levels. While boys' underachievement relative to girls' now causes considerable concern, particularly at the secondary school and higher education levels, it is the lack of male teachers, and thus the envisaged male role models for children in primary schools, that generally hits the media headlines. In 2003 the proportion of qualified male primary school teachers in England and Wales stood at 16 per cent and in Scotland at 6 per cent.

Getting more men into primary school teaching has become a *National Priority* according to *The Guardian* (Williams, 2002). The British government and individual MPs have called for more men in teaching, as role models for boys (Department for Education and Employment (DfEE), 2000; *The Observer*, July 3rd, 2005; Liam Fox MP, cited Hinsliff and Tenko 2005:13). In 2002 the TTA[1] (2002: 5) had, as one of its key targets: 'by 2002/3 recruit 20 per cent more men to train for primary teaching'. However, such a target has proved difficult to achieve.

> We continued to make progress in recruiting more men into primary teaching, 15 per cent more in 2003/04 than in the previous year. (TTA, 2004: 5)

Although more men have been recruited, there has not been an increase in the proportion of male primary teachers. Instead there has been a gradual but steady decline.

Has there ever been a golden age, when a large proportion of primary/elementary school teachers were men? Can we pinpoint any times in the last 100 years of state education when the proportion of male primary school teachers was considerably higher than it is now? Have conditions of service and recruitment methods changed? And what impact, if any, have changes in the economic, social and political climate had?

A golden age?

Public records for England and Wales from 1900 (Figure1) show that there has never been anything even close to parity in the proportions of men and women in primary teaching: in 1900 just 25 per cent (1 in 4) of elementary school teachers were men; the highest ever proportion of male elementary teachers in the last 100 years was 29 per cent (1 in 3), in 1938, and the lowest ever proportion of male primary school teachers of 16 per cent (1 in 6) was recorded in 2004.

Figure 1: Proportion of male primary/elementary school teachers and headteachers from 1900 to 2004

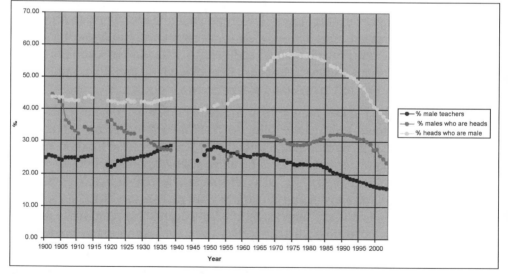

(Sources: Board of Education 1900-1944; Ministry of Education, 1944-1964; DES/DfEE 1964- 2000; DfES 2000-2004).

Only two periods in the last 100 years show an increase in the proportion of male primary/elementary school teachers, each following a low point at the end of one of the two world wars: 1920 to 1938 and 1945 to 1952. The first of these periods, 1920 to 1938, extends across the great depression (1929 to 1939) when there was a tremendous surge in unemployment, peaking at around 2.7 million jobless in Britain. The second period (1945 to 1952) began with the emergency training schemes of 1946 and 1947, when large numbers of men were recruited to teaching. By 1952, 28 per cent of primary teachers were men. These trends illustrate both the economic push of male unemployment caused by the depression and post-war demobilisation, plus the political pull of major training incentives.

However, as can be seen in Figure 1, since 1968 there has been a steady decline in the proportion of male primary school teachers; since 1975 a decline in the proportion of male headteachers, and since 1990 a decline in the proportion of male teachers who are heads. It is interesting to note that between 1980 and 1990, when the number of men in primary teaching was already in decline, that the proportion of men who obtained headships actually rose! In 2000, 41 per cent of primary headteachers were men and in 1902 the proportion was 43 per cent. In the intervening period the proportion of male heads fell below 40 per cent in only one year (in 1947, to 39.7 per cent). So, although men make up only a small proportion of the primary teaching force, they have until recently led almost half of primary schools.

In view of earlier trends it is likely that political and economic factors have had an effect and we will examine these and social factors, such as the changing nature of teaching and gender relationships over the last century.

Economic push and pull

The rise in the proportion of men in elementary/primary teaching between 1919 and 1938 and again between 1945 and 1952 must be viewed in the context of the inevitable falls during both World Wars. Both created labour shortages, with many different jobs, once considered the sole preserve of men, being filled by women. With the conscription of men, Britain had no choice but to recruit female labour to sustain the economy. During both periods women were encouraged, indeed required, to work outside the home. Nevertheless, the pre-war proportions of men and women teachers were restored by 1929 and 1952 respectively. There are obvious similarities in the changing proportion of male teachers during and after each of these two wars; a sharp decline during the war followed by a slower rise after the war. However, there are also two important differences.

The first is that after 1952 the proportion of men in teaching had reached its peak and begun to fall, whereas after 1929 the proportion continued to increase until the last pre-war records in 1938. The depression (1929-1939) with its high levels of unemployment and the increased imposition of a marriage bar, were key factors in this. During the depression women were encouraged back into the home as jobs for men became increasingly scarce and married women were barred from taking teaching jobs. In spite of the 1919 Sex Discrimination (Removal) Act women suddenly found the marriage bar being reinforced within professions such as teaching and by 1926 it was imposed by three quarters of all LEAs (Oram, 1996: Copelman, 1996).

The second difference is that the proportion of men in teaching recovered to pre-war levels faster after the Second World War than the First World World, despite the economic push of the depression. Emergency training courses for teachers were established and these probably encouraged more men to join the profession. The peak period for men in primary teaching came in 1952, after which it began its inexorable decline. This was eight years after the marriage bar had finally been removed, enabling women to continue teaching after marriage and to pursue a career with some structure and opportunities for promotion. Women joining the teaching profession in 1945, in their early twenties, might have spent a number of years in teaching before they married so it is not surprising to see a time lag of eight years before the removal of the marriage bar becomes apparent in the statistics, and the proportion of women teachers begins to increase.

In Figure 1, between 1952 and 1975, there were two opposing trends: a steady decline in the proportion of male teachers and a rapid increase in the proportion of male headteachers. Teaching had now become a viable long-term career for both single and married women: this is undoubtedly reflected in their increased numbers. However, economically, headship brings greater rewards. Quite why there was this sudden dramatic increase of around 15 per cent in the proportion of male headteachers is more difficult to explain. It is far in excess of the relatively small increase in male teachers post WW2 which was around 5 per cent whose career stage might help to explain such a bulge: the relatively high salary was clearly less inviting after 1975.

One study of headteacher appointments found that during the 1980s and early 1990s, men were selected for just over one third of primary headships; by 1993-96, they were selected for 24 per cent, and by 1998, for less than 12 per cent, close to their current proportions in the primary teaching force. (Ross, cited Budge, 1999:1). However, it was, and remains the case today that men hold, disproportionately, more of the senior posts in all sectors of education (Al-Khalifa, 1989; Jones, 1990; Southworth, 1990; Measor and Sikes, 1992; Thornton, 1999, EOC, 2005). While the proportion of men heading primary schools has declined significantly since 1975, in line with the decline in male primary teachers, our data suggest that they are still more likely than women teachers to obtain headships. We explore possible explanations for this in chapter 7.

The salary incentive?

While good prospects for promotion to headship might attract more men into teaching, the salaries earned by primary school teachers, relative to what they could earn in other occupations requiring similar levels of qualification, might be a disincentive for men. Dolton and Chung (2004) have shown that since 1975 the earnings of other occupations have risen whilst those of teachers have declined relatively. They state that men are now financially better off in occupations other than teaching whilst women are better off teaching than many other occupations.

> ... our analysis shows that teaching is not financially attractive for males while, for females, teaching still appears to be a relatively well remunerated job compared to the alternatives. (Dolton and Chung, 2004: 95)

> Males entering teaching since 2000 stand to lose an average of £67,000 worth of earnings over their lifetime if they became a primary school teacher and average earnings of £40,000 on becoming a secondary teacher. (Dolton and Chung, 2004: 99)

So salary could certainly be a factor in the post-1975 decline in the proportion of men primary teachers. The 1970 Equal Pay Act came into force in 1975, along with the Sex Discrimination Act (1975), at the same time teaching degrees were beginning to replace teaching certificates – which may also be relevant. Firstly, discrimination in pay and appointment is no longer lawful. This may have enhanced the position of women teachers, although a substantial pay and promotion gap still exists. Secondly, equal pay may have encouraged more women into teaching, and, in a more competitive environment, especially if graduate teachers were being sought by employers and if more women had these higher entry qualifications, some men may have been effectively squeezed out. Thirdly, the increasing availability of women teachers may have enabled class teacher salaries, initially attractive to men, to be suppressed to a level more in keeping with a predominantly female profession.

An alternative view might be to see the 1975 Acts as an effective pull for more men in teaching, since before this a woman teacher could be employed for less money than a man teacher but once these Acts were in operation women did not have this advantage in terms of gaining employment. Clearly this was not an effective pull.

However, once employed as teachers, there is a strong tendency for men to gain headships in larger schools (Edwards and Lyons, 1996) where salaries are higher, for men to earn more per week than women teachers (Weale, 1996), and for men to benefit from an 11 per cent pay differential when working full-time in education (EOC, 2005). Promotion to headship offers the possibility of higher salaries and men traditionally have had a greater chance of achieving this, as two male teachers recount:

> I initially trained as a secondary PE teacher and I spent ten years in the secondary phase of education before moving to primary... once you move to primary then things seem to move at a much different rate because you can become a member of the management team then you become a Deputy Head and then you become a Head. So I went from a career which was going nowhere to one that has moved on very quickly... (Male Head, Teachers' Careers)

> I've been cheered, as a male, by the fact that my career prospects appear that much better... I can come into teaching on a low salary and then three years on look for a deputy headship, maybe another four years look for a headship, and be quick about it because in that way I can move up the scale... (Tom, BEd Year 4, Men's Club)

Further work by Chung *et al* (2004: 23) indicates that graduate unemployment has a significant influence on teacher supply in the UK and that this is stronger for men than for women: higher levels of unemployment lead to an increase in the proportion of graduates entering Initial Teacher Training (ITT) programmes. This can be mapped against our time line in Figure 1. Unemployment levels peaked in 1932 and in 1986 and have since then fallen (Hicks and Allen, 1999). Post 1986 the proportion of male teachers fell. If high unemployment is the key, an economic downturn may bring more men back into teaching. It also possible that the pendulum effect of teachers' salaries which catch up, fall back and catch up again, may be more off-putting for men than for women.

Politics and teaching

Our exploration of the changing proportions of men and women in primary school teaching over the last century indicates that economic factors have been important, most notably the depression, war and the subsequent requirement to expand male employment opportunities. We have seen both pushes and pulls for men and women contemplating entering the teaching professions. However, it is often direct political acts that impact on education, sometimes in unexpected ways.

The 1918 Education Act after the First World War meant that all children had to attend school until the age of fourteen, thus creating the need for more teachers, while at the same time the marriage bar prevented married women from taking these jobs. Figure 1 illustrates the increase in male teachers at this time.

The 1944 Education Act signalled the end of the elementary school which catered for pupils up to age fourteen and the birth of the primary school for pupils up to the age of eleven, alongside compulsory secondary schooling. There has been a steady and unremitting decline in the proportion of male primary school teachers since the early 1950s and this may be explained in part by the change in educational age phases brought about by the 1944 Act. Research indicates that men disproportionately teach older children in all age phases (Bricheno and Thornton, 2002; Thornton, 1999a; Hutchings, 2002a) whether through appointment, direction or personal choice. The oldest children taught in the new primary schools are eleven whereas in elementary schools it was fourteen, thus becoming a possible deterrent for men from teaching, at least in primary schools. At the same time the removal of the marriage bar in 1945 (McNair, 1944) allowed greater competition for teaching positions and for career moves, effectively creating another deterrent for men and an important new attraction for women.

The later introduction of first, middle and upper schools in 1967, alongside primary and secondary schools, presented opportunities for subject specialist teaching (Thornton, 1998) of eight to thirteen year olds without the requirement to move into the secondary sector to do so. Our research suggests that the opportunity to teach their own subject is a strong motivator for both male and female teachers but that it is stronger for men (Reid and Thornton, 2000). However, this potential attraction for men did not result in increased numbers after 1967.

Between 1975 and 1985, a period during which there was a surplus of primary school teachers in some areas and many teacher training colleges were closed or amalgamated, the proportion of male primary school teachers remained relatively stable. Only after 1986 did the decline begin again in earnest. The proportion of male teachers slipped below the 20 per cent mark in 1990, two years after the ERA 1988 (DES, 1989) was introduced, and has continued to decline ever since.

The ERA was a substantial piece of legislation that fundamentally changed the structure and control of education in England and Wales. From the Plowden report (DES,1967) which advocated that children should be at the heart of the curriculum in decentralised state schools under the control of class teachers, headteachers and LEAs, there was a shift to a compulsory National Curriculum (NC) with core and foundation subjects at its heart, centrally prescribed and controlled, irrespective of newly devolved local management of schools, and an ever-increasing, suffocating focus on assessment, accountability and performance measured through national tests, school league tables, Ofsted (Office for Standards in Education) inspections and performance-related pay for teachers. Teacher performance is publicised through their pupils' test scores and failure is punished.

By 1990 not only had the percentage of male teachers dropped below 20 per cent for the first time but the proportion of men headteachers also began to fall even more dramatically (Figure 1), from more than 50 per cent to less than 40 per cent over a ten year period from 1991 to 2001. More recent Government initiatives that have changed teacher training and recruitment methods (see chapter 5) and incentives for career development, such as fast-track progression through the salary scale and appointment as advanced skills teachers (see chapter 7) have not arrested the now marked decline in the numbers of male primary school teachers.

Changing society, changing teachers

Through a social, rather than an economic or political lens, we can see that perhaps there never was a Golden Age before men went missing and primary schools had more male teachers. We have seen that, since 1900, it was never the case that the majority of primary school teachers were male, but there was a time when men held considerably more power within the primary school than is the case today.

During the 20th century women gradually gained more rights in law, some of which have been identified above. Formally, if not always in practice, they now have equal rights in almost all occupational and social fields. They hold the majority of headships in primary schools, there are many female school governors and some powerful women making political decisions in the DfES.

In the 1970s, gender equality issues came to the fore, via new legislation, government concerns over economic needs, and a perception in some quarters that the talents of at least some girls were not being fully exploited. The EOC effectively promoted gender equality in education and in society, and second wave feminism's concern with discrimination and girls' then relative underachievement in education also had an impact. With the support of feminist teachers and government initiatives, such as girls into science (Whyte, 1984), the education of girls, and women's subsequent careers, became salient social issues. By the 1980s, the gender equality battle in schools was thought to have been won by politicians and, in the 1990s, girls were perceived not only to have closed the gender gap but to be overtaking boys (Arnot *et al*, 1999). A public panic about boys' so-called underachievement coupled with decreasing numbers of male teachers then ensued.

Now there are suggestions that the balance of power has shifted in education. Whilst, as we have demonstrated, there has never been a golden age of a male majority in teaching, there are increasing accusations that education has become 'feminised' (Skelton, 2002: 85) and that this explains the decline in men in teaching, the gender gap in boys' and girls' achievements, and increasing problems with boys' behaviour. What is the basis for such claims? And if education has become feminised, what are the implications of this for men in education?

There certainly have been significant changes in the schooling of boys and girls, the curricula they study and assessment practices. Following Hadow (1926) and reinforced by Plowden (DES, 1967), children were deemed to be at the heart of the curriculum. Subjects were taught but, in theory if not always in practice (Thornton, 1995), the curriculum followed the needs and interests of children (Sharpe and Green, 1975).

The backlash against Plowden's progressive education came almost immediately, typified by the publication of a series of papers collectively known as the *Black Papers* (Cox and Dyson, 1969 and 1975; Cox, and Boyson, 1971 and 1977), but it was not until the 1980s that a conservative government took up these concerns and began to intervene directly in the functioning of schools. HM Inspectorate's Report, *A View of the Curriculum*, initiated consultation on policies for the curriculum (DES, 1980) and this was followed by *The School Curriculum* which recommended a broad curriculum up to age sixteen (DES, 1981).

The ERA 1988, with its nationally prescribed curriculum for all, ensured that boys and girls would all study the same subjects until the age of sixteen, that subjects were at the heart of the curriculum (Alexander, 1984; Alexander *et al*, 1992), and that all teachers, including primary, should be subject specialists. National tests were introduced at age seven, eleven and thirteen to be followed by league tables and prescribed teaching methods (the literacy and numeracy hours). Whilst formal assessment was dramatically increased and became overtly competitive with league tables at GCSE level, assessment through coursework, rather than final examination also increased.

Alongside these structural changes there is now much debate about boys' achievements in relation to girls, and considerably more assertion than evidence that male teachers might or do make a difference to boys' achievements. Educational research and publications have been silent regarding the impact men, as teachers and role models, might have on the perceptions and educational experiences of pupils, their achievements and their behaviour. Given the weight and extent of educational and school-based research into boys' achievements compared with girls', government policy to raise standards, and TDA strategies to recruit more men, it is remarkable how rarely teacher gender has been addressed as a variable within school-based educational research and school improvement initiatives.

Boys' achievements relative to girls'

How boys' and girls' achievements have changed over the last century is not easy to assess, partly because of changes in assessment methods and partly because of the scarcity of national test data over these years.

Current concerns about boys' underachievement in relation to girls' are partly due to changes in assessment methods, which now allow comparisons over time. Comparison of Key Stage Test (KST) and

GCSE results year on year is being used to demonstrate the increasing underachievement of boys in relation to girls. This is only possible because assessment was changed[2] in 1988 from norm-referencing, allocating grades in proportion to the entry cohort, to criterion-referencing, allocating grades in terms of skills and competencies. The norm-referencing system of assessment was unable to detect improvement in performance over time; grades were allocated proportionately and simply discriminated between the performances of students in one cohort at a time. Student performance may have been improving prior to 1988. We have no way of judging. Since 1988 there is evidence of change over time: the entry cohort for examinations has increased as a proportion of the age cohort, and the grades awarded are improving year-on-year. However, caution should be exercised. Clearly we need to consider the possibility of the distortion of such performance indicators (Fitz-Gibbon, 1996).

> Where norm-referencing is not used, and scores are allowed to increase annually there is a danger of producing 'counterfeit excellence'. In the USA high school grades have improved over time but without any linked rise in student academic achievement measured by independent measures of attainment (ACT Assessment). This has been confirmed in several studies, sometimes leading to a 'Lake Wobegon effect' where everyone is declared 'above average' in attainment (Zirkel, 1999)! (cited Gorard and Taylor, 2001:9)

Before the introduction of Key Stage Tests in 1994 the only large-scale tests of primary school children were the 11+ examinations, taken by all pupils in their last year at primary school from 1944 until 1970, when many but not all schools became comprehensive. Since these were prescribed by individual LEAs, they could not be said to be national tests. However, there are indications that girls outperformed boys in the 11+ examinations (Gipps and Murphy, 1994), suggesting that the gender gap is not a recent phenomenon and that girls were doing better than boys, even though men were more often to be found teaching in, and heading, primary schools at that time.

In the 1960s and 70s the current preoccupation with standards and testing did not exist and national tests were uncommon. There is some data from various large-scale one-off surveys of reading, English and Mathematics. These surveys of children aged eleven indicated small and mainly insignificant differences between boys and girls in Reading, English and Mathematics (DES, 1967; Douglas *et al*, 1968; HMI, 1978; Gorman *et al*, 1988). Certainly there is no evidence to indicate that boys were doing significantly better than girls when there were a greater proportion of male primary teachers as role models.

Towards the end of the 1970s there was increased pressure for accountability in the sense that systems, schools and teachers were increasingly required to demonstrate that students were meeting standards. The Assessment of Performance Unit (APU) was set up

> to promote the development of methods of assessing and monitoring the achievement of children in school and seek to identify the incidence of underachievement. (DES 1974, cited Gipps and Murphy, 1994:114).

The surveys took place between 1975 and 1989, covering a wide range of tests in various subjects, but only English and Mathematics continued throughout the whole period. The APU found that girls consistently outperformed boys in English and that boys only did consistently better than girls in a single aspect of the Mathematics tests. In addition they noted that girls improved their performance in relation to boys between 1978 and 1982, showing them to be ahead of boys in Mathematics in 1982. This limited evidence suggests that in primary schools boys were not doing significantly better than girls during the 40s, 50s and 60s, the so-called golden age of the male primary school teacher.

Since the introduction of KST changes year on year differences between boys and girls have become easy to see. However, despite the fall in the proportion of men in primary teaching, there is no obvious transformation in the gender gap overall. Girls are really outperforming boys only in English, as has long been the case. In other areas boys and girls aged eleven seem to be performing at similar levels: the DfES (2005a) notes that

> ... the standard of achievement for all pupils has been rising since the 1980s but because of the differential rates of improvements, girls are still performing better than boys. Nationally, girls outperform boy's at all four key stages in English. The position in mathematics up to the age of sixteen seems to be more evenly matched and in science there are signs that girls have begun to fall behind by age eleven.

Such evidence suggests that the assertion that boys are only now underachieving in comparison to girls at age eleven is unjustified.

There is more substantial evidence available of the achievements of boys and girls at the end of secondary school. Comparison of the old

GCE 'O' level results and the new GCSE results for those obtaining five or more A-C grades can give us some idea of any change over time for those aged sixteen years. Figure 2 shows the percentage of boys and girls achieving five or more A-C GCSE grades or their equivalent from 1962 to 2004 (DfES, 2005b): for reference purposes the proportion of male secondary school teachers has been included on the same figure.

Figure 2: Trends in GCE/GCSE results and proportion of male secondary school teachers 1962-2004

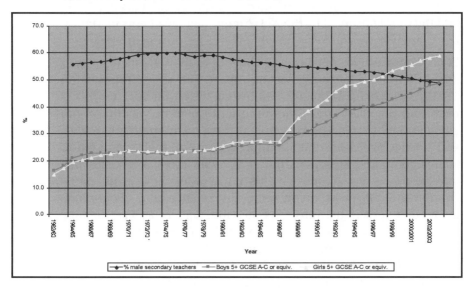

At the bottom left hand corner of Figure 2 it can be seen that in 1962 boys were doing better than girls, but only about 16 per cent of boys and about 15 per cent of girls were achieving five or more good grades in GCE 'O' level examinations. This proportion has increased over the years until by 2004 almost 50 per cent of boys compared with almost 60 per cent of girls had five or more GCSE passes at A-C or above. During this same period the proportion of full-time male secondary school teachers has fallen from about 55 per cent to just below 50 per cent.

Between 1962 and 1975 boys' attainment levels rose and during the same period girls caught up, until from 1970 to 1980 boys and girls were achieving at similar levels. This happened at a time when the proportion of male secondary school teachers was increasing. A very small female advantage first became apparent in 1981, and after 1987 increased rapidly until 1994. Since 1994, the difference between boys and girls has remained fairly constant and although the proportion of both genders achieving five or more good grades at GCSE has increased, the difference between them has not.

In summary, the available evidence shows that levels of attainment by both boys and girls at age sixteen have risen very substantially over the past forty years. Average levels of attainment by boys have increased, although not as much as girls' averages. At age eleven the evidence is less clear-cut but there are indications that girls have done better than boys for many years. Explanations of gender differences in attainment therefore need to take account of factors not of recent origin, and in view of the discontinuity in Figure 2 in 1988, and the trend observed by the APU for girls achievements in Mathematic in 1982, we will focus on what increased during the 1980s.

Equal opportunities policies and changes in the school curriculum are likely to have had a significant impact. The Sex Discrimination Act 1975 encouraged equality initiatives in the curriculum, examinations and the classroom. One important outcome was that more girls enrolled for a wider range of subjects including Mathematics and Science, which resulted in improvements in their examination results compared to boys (Arnot *et al*, 1996, 1999). The 1980s was marked by a research focus on girls' curriculum choices and, particularly, their level of involvement in Science and Technology inspired by such initiatives as the Girls into Science and Technology project in the early 1980s. Government also addressed the problem of gendered subject choices in secondary education. The Technical and Vocational Education Initiative (TVEI), begun in 1984, had the explicit objective of promoting gender equality (Tinklin et al, 2001). It set out to improve the technological and vocational relevance of the school curriculum, but also aimed to reduce gender stereotypes with regard to subject choice and career aspirations. The later introduction of a common examination system in 1986, and a compulsory National Curriculum (ERA, DES, 1989) both focused on gender equity in subject choice, making it compulsory for boys to study Modern Languages and for girls to study Mathematics, Science and Technology. These major changes, during the 1980s may serve as a better explanation of girls' improved achievements in relation to boys than the fall in the percentage of male teachers.

Teachers' gender and achievement

There are few research studies that have considered the effect of the gender of the teachers on the achievement of boys and girls. What little there is falls into one of two categories: studies examining the views of students about the quality of teaching they receive and analyses of survey data including examination or test results.

Interviews with 90 students aged thirteen to fourteen from Finland suggest that the gender of the teacher has little impact on the quality of the teaching (Lahelma, 2000). Wragg *et al* (2000) interviewed 519 pupils aged six to sixteen about what makes a good or bad teacher; the children are not reported as mentioning the gender of the teacher as important. However, Jules and Kutnik (1997) analysed essays and interviews from 1756 children aged eight to sixteen years in Trinidad and Tobago, concerning student perceptions of a good teacher, and suggest that all young children may prefer to be taught by a female teacher.

The Finnish research involved a small group of secondary students, and that of Wragg *et al* (2000) involved only 46 children aged six years, the rest being eleven years and above, so it may be that the views of the younger pupils were not well represented in these studies. On the other hand, the larger sample of Jules and Kutnik (1992), although more representative of the relevant age group, involved children from a different culture. In none of these studies is there any suggestion that a male teacher was particularly important but Brutsart and Bracke (1994) suggest that the gender composition of the teaching staff does exert an influence on pupils: girls did not appear to be affected by the gender organisation of the school, but boys' school commitment levels were negatively affected by a high proportion of female teachers. This research, which is not as yet supported by other studies, involved a large sample (2095 pupils) but as it is a sub-set of the original sample and includes only private Roman Catholic schools, it may be unrepresentative, and there may also be cultural/religious explanations for their findings.

Survey data is similarly contradictory. The Plowden Report (DES, 1967) suggests that boys appear to do slightly better with women teachers and girls substantially better. It is worth noting that this study of children in England and Wales took place at a time when the proportion of male teachers in primary schools was considerably higher than today (26%).

In the United States, Ehrenberg *et al* (1995) have used data from the National Educational Longitudinal Study of 1988 to show that teacher gender has little impact on the achievements of boys or girls. Our own research (Bricheno and Thornton, 2002) suggests that, in primary school at least, boys' and girls' achievements are unrelated to the proportions of male and female teachers, although there is a suggestion that Maths achievements may be slightly enhanced in schools with a male headteacher. Again, the evidence is limited and conflicting but all these studies indicate that any gender-based differences are small.

More recently Carrington *et al* (2005), in a large study in English primary schools, using attitude questionnaires and attainment scores for children from 413 separate classes of eleven year olds (113 taught by males and 300 by females) during the 1997/8 academic year, found no empirical evidence to support the claim that more male teachers might enhance the educational achievement of boys. They also found that children, both boys and girls, taught by women were more inclined to show positive attitudes towards school than those taught by men.

Teachers' gender and pupil behaviour

In contrast to pervasive assumptions about the absence of men impacting on boys' achievements, there is a wealth of research evidence to suggest that differences between boys' and girls' behaviour has been a perennial issue. The Taunton Commission, 1868, stated that 'Girls come to you to learn; boys have to be driven', while the Board of Education, 1923, (cited Cohen, 1998: 27) claimed '... it is well known that most boys, especially in the period of adolescence, have a habit of 'healthy idleness'.'

In a review of primary school behaviour Davies (1984) indicated that boys' behaviour was more problematic than girls' and that research throughout the 60s and 70s had found this to be the case. Croll and Moses (1990) make the same observation about research conducted in the 1980s: boys' behaviour in primary school was found to be less good than that of girls, while Stake and Katz, (1982) found that women teachers gave more encouragement and praise and less reprimands than men teachers. Similarly Howe (1997), reviewing studies in the 1990s, finds that boys misbehave more than girls. Recent surveys by Whitelaw *et al* (2000) and Younger *et al* (1999) find that girls are less likely to be punished for poor behaviour than boys. Interestingly, women teachers appear to evaluate boys' behaviour more positively than men teachers (Hopf, and Hatzichristou, 1999). A Scottish study (Munn *et al*, 1990) identified a wide range of discipline strategies and found that no single category dominated the data; strictness, shouting, threatening and warning made up only 16 per cent of the comments. While these researchers had not set out to examine the relationship between teacher gender and strategies for classroom control, gender was attached to the examples they gave i.e. for strategies such as being very strict and getting very angry, the quotes were all from male teachers, but examples of help, encouragement, praise and rewards were all from women.

Many transfer studies show that boys' attitudes to school decline more than girls' on moving from primary to secondary school (Bricheno, 2001; Galton *et al*, 1999; Keys *et al*, 1995; Huggins and Knight, 1997; Murdoch, 1986; Spelman, 1979). Could this attitude decline be related to the increase in the proportion of male teachers in secondary schools? Our own recent research into Ofsted reports suggests that behaviour is deemed better in primary schools with a greater proportion of women – i.e. no unsatisfactory behaviour was observed in sample schools with an all-female staff (Appendix A7; chapter 7), and The Annual Report by the Chief Inspector (Ofsted, 2005a) reported that in primary schools:

> Pupils' attitudes to school are almost always positive and behaviour is good. Schools generally work hard to promote good relationships and almost all deal successfully with bullying and racism (Paragraph 32)

> ... the proportion of good or better behaviour in secondary schools has declined from over three quarters to two thirds and there has been no reduction in the proportion of unsatisfactory behaviour (just under one school in 10). (Paragraph 127)

These findings could signify that pupil behaviour is affected by the gender of the teacher, boys' behaviour being negatively affected by male teachers; they certainly do not support the view that more men in schools leads to an improvement in boys' behaviour. However, the evidence available is quite limited and further research is needed to explore this question.

At times boys' misbehaviour has been celebrated (Willis, 1977; Corrigan, 1979) as a rejection of the imposition of middle-class educational values on working-class youth. Whilst still heavily class related, it is now termed 'laddishness' (Francis, 2000) and recognised as a problem for government, girls' education in school and boys' future employability. Whether boys' behaviour has actually deteriorated over time is difficult to prove. The continuing rise in boys' and girls' exclusions (Osler and Vincent, 2003) suggest that it has deteriorated, but this may relate to other changes such as increased accountability, public measures of performance, such as league tables and an inspection regime which penalises schools that tolerate poor pupil behaviour.

Is teaching feminised?

There is strong evidence that concerns about the behaviour of boys and the current so-called feminisation of teaching are not new:

> American Psychologist Dr Stanley Hall was often cited [in the 1930s] as having proved that women's influence promoted juvenile de-linquency. Dr Hall wrote, 'I believe that the progressive feralization of boys, the growing hoodlism etc., of which all complain, is directly connected with the feminization of home and school'.

> The pernicious influence of women teachers on boys was a frequent theme of NAS [National Association of School Masters] thinking. At its 1930 Conference, Mr Gordon of London wanted boys to be taught by 'the most manly type of teacher available' and Mr Free-borough of Banstead feared that 'they could not feminize 700,000 boys without feminizing the nation. Then we should soon begin to sink lower than other nations (Cheers)'. (Partington, 1976:41-42)

Current claims about the feminisation of teaching are based on several things. The predominance of women teachers is one but we have shown that women have always been in the majority and the decline between 1990 and 2000 in male primary teachers of less than five per cent, and in male secondary teachers of less than three per cent, hardly seems an appropriate basis for such claims. If teaching is indeed feminised purely on the basis of numbers, then it must have been feminised for the past 100 years, including the long period when boy's achievements at age sixteen exceeded those of girls and the current period when their achievements have clearly improved albeit not as fast as those of girls.

The change in power relationships might be more salient, namely an increase in the proportion of women headteachers in primary schools from 49 to 60 per cent over the same period. But this is un-likely to have affected gendered educational outcomes in any causal way, given dramatically increased centralised government control of content and direction on pedagogy during the same period.

Another claim to feminisation rests upon the increased use of coursework in formal assessment. In principle this allows time for reflection and revision and is thought to favour girls' preference for timely consideration and weighing of arguments. Short, sharp, timed, competitive examinations are thought to favour boys.

> Boys show greater adaptability to more traditional approaches to learning which require the memorisation of abstract, unambiguous facts and rules that have to be acquired quickly. They also appear to

be more willing to sacrifice deep understanding which requires effort, for correct answers achieved at speed. (Arnot *et al*, 1998:28)

While this may go some way to explaining girls' increasing success in GCSE examinations, it hardly denotes a feminisation of assessment, where timed examinations still play a major part in overall grades and outcomes.

Yet another claim to feminisation rests upon teaching style and curriculum content. There is much current work that suggests that boys prefer short sharp bursts of activity in lessons and content shaped towards their interests, stereotypically, mechanical rather than emotional, sport rather than artistic endeavours, competition rather than collaborative working (Biddulph, 1997; Mills, 2000; Noble, 1998). But it is difficult to see how style and content may have changed in favour of feminine approaches over such a short period of time, under a centrally prescribed subject-based curriculum. Again, claims that it has always been so because of the pre-dominance of women teachers, and assumed prior pervasiveness of Plowden's nurturing teachers and teaching style, might carry greater weight than those currently offered for boys much more recent relative underachievement in relation to girls.

When we consider the trends of the last 100 years the accusation of feminisation is not justified. Rather, it is more likely to be an example of *backlash politics* (Skelton, 2002: 86). The majority of teachers have always been female, and education, the curriculum, teaching styles and assessment have, if anything, become consider-ably more *masculinised* through an emphasis on testing and assess-ment, performance indicators, and stratified and hierarchical management and administration structures (Arnot and Miles, 2005).

What are the implications of this for men in education? Surely, if education is being masculinised, boys' achievements relative to girls should be increasing and teaching should be a more attractive career for men. It does seem strange that when masculine features of education are in the ascendance there is a steady and continuing decline in the number of men teachers. Is it related to other social factors such as teacher status, salary, abuse implications or paedophilia awareness, or to changing power relationships such as increased female headships, associated with improvements in women's opportunities to gain headships (Wylie, 2000).

Contrasts and contradictions

As countries decentralise education administration, the role of head-teacher has increasingly emphasised management more than teaching. Decentralisation to the school level in England has greatly increased workloads as well as management responsibilities for headteachers. In some senses this fits better with a stereotypical masculine view of teachers' work. Rather than the care and nurturing of women who deliver progressive education (Sharp and Green, 1975; DES, 1967), teachers' work now is structured, planned, organised, managed, controlled and evaluated in accord with asserted male preferences but contrary to perceived women's preferences (Mahony et al, 2004). Schools are also becoming increasingly masculinised through the emphasis on testing and assessment, performance indicators, and hierarchical management and administration structures (Arnot and Miles, 2005).

Rather than supporting assertions that teaching has become feminised, the ERA and its subsequent development has effectively masculinised the educational environment, far beyond management structures and teachers career pathways (Mahony et al, 2004b). Women remain the front line workers in schools but why and for how long? As a so-called semi- profession teachers are deemed in need of control (see chapter 4), and in the current situation this will be through centralised bureaucratic controls. Men in centrally powerful roles can manage this without needing to be physically at the chalk face in schools and classrooms. Direction and control is what really matters, that is where the power over education lies. Alternatively, men might actually return to teaching in greater numbers in the future, given its increasingly masculine traits and characteristics.

Changes in the wider economic, social and political spheres may have caused the gradual decline in the numbers of men in teaching that we have shown in this chapter. So too might the significant changes that have taken place in education over the past 100 years, with men rejecting rather than laying claim to newer, masculinised styles of organisation, monitoring and content. However, what cannot be reasonably claimed, is that this relative and definitely recent decline in the numbers of male teachers has actually caused education to become feminised or caused poorer behaviour amongst boys. Nor is it responsible for boys' current relative and recent underachievement when compared to girls.

Recommended reading

Penny Harnett (2003) has conducted a similar historical study of the proportions of men and women teachers over the past century. Harnett, P. (2003) Where have all the men gone? Have primary schools really been feminised? *Journal of Educational Administration and History*, Vol 35, no 2 pp77-86

Madeline Arnot, Miriam David and Gaby Weiner's overview of post-WW2 changes in gender patterns in education provides a detailed account of the social context in which changes in boys' and girls' academic achievements can be located. Arnot, M. David, M. and Weiner, G. (1999) *Closing the Gender Gap: Postwar Education and Social Change*, Cambridge: Polity Press. Chapter 2, p12-30.

4
Teaching as a Career Choice: why not for men?

Introduction

Mills (2005:5) summarises the most common reasons offered within the literature for why men don't teach. He refers directly to primary schools but the reasons offered generally relate to all levels of education. They relate to the low status of teachers,

> ... poor wages in relation to the work performed; limited career path for those not seeking administrative roles; the labelling of male primary school teachers as homosexual or not 'real men'; the current media spotlight on allegations of child abuse; the fear of being labelled a paedophile.

We will address most of these reasons in this chapter, through exploring teaching as a career choice. This is fundamental to understanding male absence from teaching: why don't they become teachers in the first place? Subsequent chapters examine what happens to those that do.

Jobs and work places are sexed and gendered, not neutral spaces (Cockburn, 1983, 1985, 1991). Headlines such as *Only the boys boot up* (*THES*, 2005:6) and *Why girls don't tap into plumbing* (Lepkowska, 2005:14) confirm the existence and continuation of this sexual division of labour. Its cause may well be the pervasiveness of gender stereotypes that influence young people's career choices. These come from peers, family, or even, unfortunately, via teachers themselves and the careers services (Thornton and Reid, 2001; Reid and Thornton, 2000). It is consolidated by work placement experience for fourteen to eighteen year olds – which overwhelmingly reinforces traditional occupational choices. The Equal Opportunities Commission (EOC, cited Lepkowska, 2005) suggest that in 1999 just one third of careers services had sound equal opportunity policies. While the EOC views work experience as the key to careers education in schools, it argues for more taster courses and for the Careers Service (CS) to encourage clients to enter non-traditional areas. It found in its survey of CS provision that 'there are indications that gender stereotyping influences decisions over placements and this may be a lost opportunity' (p6).

Strategies to overcome gender-stereotyped career choices usually recommend non-traditional work experience placements for both boys and girls but these remain largely unsuccessful because they are rarely implemented. Gender typical choices continue to be made by all involved, not just the young people themselves but also by many of their advisers!

At the societal level, hegemonic masculinity imposes restrictions on career options for men (Mac an Ghaill, 1994; Kenway and Willis, 1998; Connell, 1987). To make a counter-stereotypical career choice, such as teaching, requires boys and men to be particularly confident about their masculinity, to be able to cope with both the disapproval of peers and significant others in their immediate environment and the homophobic slurs on their masculinity which may follow, either directly delivered or made manifest in social commentaries. Given their current high profile as objects of scrutiny (see chapter 1) and the demands of hegemonic masculinity, it is not surprising to find that now, if not previously, men are more gender sensitive than women when it comes to career choice (Johnston *et al*, 1998).

Such constraints remain powerful despite significant change in society's expectations of men, especially so-called *new* men, who are expected to play a greater role in parenting and child care than in the past, to share domestic tasks traditionally designated women's work and to be in touch with the feminine aspects of their identities. It should be but a few small steps from here to viewing teaching as an increasingly acceptable career choice for men, but it is not. Pye *et al* (1996) ethnographic study of sixteen to eighteen year old working-class boys suggests that as one particular sub-group of men, they retain traditional views about appropriate male work, careers and family life.

Teaching as feminine work in a masculine society

Bradley (1993:11) outlines the history and centrality in feminist scholarship of occupational sex-typing and its importance in our 'understanding of gender relations and of power disparities between men and women'. Whilst we can recognise significant variation in gendered occupations across time and place, what remains common is that its incidence is 'widespread and pervasive'. Unlike some other occupations, teaching has long been and remains a predominantly female occupation in the English speaking western world and beyond.

Teaching, especially primary teaching, is almost always constructed as feminised. While we are not alone in disputing simplistic characterisations of teaching as feminine (Ashley and Lee, 2003), the disproportionate number of women teachers, together with argument that, especially in primary schools, 'the daily routines and educational practices favour females' (Delamont, 1999, cited Carrington, 2002: 288), seems to support a commonly held view within academic circles and the popular media, that teaching is indeed a feminised occupation. There are three key questions here:

■ Is teaching merely labelled feminised because of the disproportionate number of women teachers at the chalk face, and is it this designation, regardless of practice, that deters men?

■ Does teaching require teachers to exhibit so-called feminine traits, such as care for children and mothering skills and if so does this account for the absence of men?

■ Is the content, typical activity and teaching and learning style biased toward the feminine, and if so does this account for the relative underachievement of boys and the absence of men?

In each case there is a derogatory feel about the use of the term *feminised.*

Professional versus feminised care and practice

Mills, (2005:6) citing King, argues that

> Misogynist discourses have been evident in the way that primary school teaching has been constructed as a 'caring' profession, in contrast to being an 'intellectual' profession.

Care for others is seen as a predominantly female trait, although many men and male teachers exhibit this characteristic. Care is closely associated with mothering and teaching has long been characterised as a caring profession, akin to mothering (Steedman, 1985). There can be no doubt that children, whether in the home or at school, need high quality carers (Bowlby, 1953), but we agree with Ashley and Lee (2003) that the nature and foci of care is fundamentally different between the two spheres. In the home it is caring for the whole child, their physical and psychological well-being; in school it is caring about and facilitating the child's learning. Seeing the whole child is important for the teacher when other factors, such as health or family circumstances, affect the child's learning but it is a different duty of care, requiring practices which are professionally, not parentally, determined.

The ferocious debate about men working with young children often hinges on physical contact. Children need and benefit from such contact with their carers. If it is essential to the quality of their learning male and female teachers must be allowed to do it equally. But is it? We can find no research evidence that children learn better in classes where they sit on laps or get hugs and cuddles from their teachers. It does not appear in lists of traits exhibited by high quality teachers or in TDA standards, nor is it we believe general practice amongst most teachers, be they women or men.

Our research (Thornton, 1995) suggests that daily practice in classrooms, even so-called child centred ones, is far more formal, professional, curriculum-centred and gender neutral. It requires teaching not parenting skills. What exactly is deemed feminine in Ofsted's descriptions of high quality teaching and learning environments (for example, Ofsted, 2005b), or in reading stories or poems to children, encouraging imagination, artistic endeavours and musical abilities? Or in the even more common and prescribed delivery of literacy and numeracy hours and national curriculum subjects? Is group work or collaborative learning really any more feminine than individual or rote learning? Is course work really more feminine than short tests and timed examinations? Some of these daily practices, despite having a long history of co-existence in schools, and of not impeding boys' achievements in the past, are now blamed for boys' relative underachievement and labelled feminine. In the current panic about boys a scapegoat is required: so-called feminised teaching practices.

Teaching isn't mothering or caring in a parental way, any more than its actual practice is feminised but such labelling may well deter men from teaching and partly explain their absence. To describe teaching as mothering and feminised is derogatory. It disparages women as mothers, it denigrates women teachers, and it disparages teaching as a career. It is a feature of patriarchal societies. Whilst conceived as such the constraints on men entering teaching are huge and this is one of the major impediments to recruiting more men (Carrington, 2002: 301). However there is no parallel negativity in the frequent calls for more masculinised teaching practices, for more male teachers, or for male teachers to perform fathering type roles for troubled boys raised by lone women.

Teachers are predominantly women, so it is assumed that the work of teachers must be founded on stereotypical feminine traits, such as caring and mothering skills, so that teaching will inevitably be seen as women's work, accessible only to non-hegemonic sub-ordinate males. We have argued that this is not the case. It is professional and intellectual work suited to both men and women who have the necessary training and individual, personal skills, and these are definitely not gender specific. Despite current centralised control over a prescribed curriculum, forcefully advocated teaching strategies, and external policing of conformity, standards through Ofsted, and high stakes external assessment, the high proportion of women in teaching permits the simplistic deduction that it must be feminine in its key features, even if the evidence suggests that it is not. The designation feminine, whether real or imaginary, will deter the kind of men who construct their masculine identities around 'not being female' (Kimmel, 1994; Connell, 1987; Epstein, 1997). Another media headline says it all: *Ladies' job' tag deters recruits* (Mansell, 2000: 1).

We agree with Mills (2005:6) that the reasons for male absence from teaching cannot be understood 'without a consideration of misogyny and homophobia', to which we would add patriarchy. These he suggests 'are integral to the devaluing of teaching and of the gendered construction of the teaching force.' The low status of teaching is not caused by women's presence *per se* but rather by 'the status accorded to women in society' (Acker, 1994:84), so that teacher status is constrained by patriarchy and borders on misogyny.

Acker (1994:81) notes that, 'Much of the literature on school teachers reflects a lack of respect, if not outright contempt, for their intellectual abilities'. She quotes Langveld (1963) and Morrish (1978) respectively to illustrate this negativity against women (Acker, 1994:85).

> ... no country should pride itself on its educational systems if the teaching profession has become predominantly a world of women.

> ... there can be little doubt that in the past much of the sense of a second-rate profession attached to teaching has been the fact that it was predominantly female in membership.

Delamont (1999: 14) calls it

> The discourse of derision aimed at women teachers (which) blames them for failing to provide an abrasive atmosphere suited to challenge boys.

In her historical review of the literature Acker found that women teachers were discussed mainly in relation to their family roles, as to whether they were married and had children, and that a deficit model of women as teachers was produced: male experience was taken as the norm against which women were 'then (unfavourably) compared' (Acker, 1994:80).

She cites Simpson and Simpson (1969: 199-200) to illustrate the ways in which women teachers are negatively caricatured, defined against the male norm, in need of control and why they have only themselves to blame for their low status and the low status of teaching in general.

> A woman's primary attachment is to the family role; women are therefore less intrinsically committed to work than men and less likely to maintain a high level of specialized knowledge. Because their work motives are more utilitarian and less intrinsically task oriented than those of men, they may require more control ... they often share the general cultural norm that women should defer to men, (such that) women are more willing than men to accept the bureaucratic controls imposed upon them in semi-professional organisations, and less likely to seek a genuinely professional status.

While perhaps less overt nowadays, because of teacher supply and retention issues, the negative connotations of teaching as women's work persist, in the then Secretary of State John Patten's call for a 'Mum's Army', in David Blunkett's description of the four-year BEd as a 'sub-degree undergraduate course' (cited McAvoy, 2000:23), or in TDA advertisements aimed at men emphasising stereotypical male traits such as intellect, science and sport.

Alongside misogynist and patriarchal views of teaching lie homophobic ones. These suggest that men who teach cannot be *real* men because real men don't engage in activities characterised as feminine activities, such as work with children. If they are not real men then they must be paedophiles or gay (Mills, 2005). As Sargent (2001: 19) notes, 'Men who do not fit the mould of hegemonic masculinity are looked upon with suspicion or even considered dangerous.'

Homophobic discourse marginalises men who teach for failing to conform to the rules of hegemonic masculinity and is a serious deterrent to men entering teaching, especially primary teaching. Men who make teaching their career choice go against the grain of mainstream expectation.

At the macro level misogyny, patriarchy and homophobia construct teaching as feminine, although, as we argued in chapter 3, at the meso and micro levels of schools and classrooms, it seems to have become distinctly masculinised. Without work experience potential recruits to teaching will not see teaching as it really is, and the macro level designation of teaching as feminine and therefore not for men, will prevail.

Teaching as low status

Teaching is seen as a low status occupation because of its designation as feminine and because the majority of its workers are female. Similarly, recent increases in the numbers of women training to be doctors has led to concern that medicine as a profession will lose status and become feminised, as evidenced in the newspaper headline, *Medical time-bomb: too many women doctors* (Laurance, 2004: 1).

A major DfES funded project, *The Status of Teachers and the Teaching Profession* is currently underway in Cambridge, directed by Linda Hargreaves. Interim finding (Hargreaves *et al*, 2004) confirm that concerns about the status of teaching are perennial, not least amongst teachers themselves. Most teachers in the first survey saw high status accruing to occupations that commanded authority, autonomy, respect, remuneration and responsibility, whereas teaching was characterised 'by strong external control, and little reward and respect' (p16). Gender differences revolved around strength of feeling about these issues.

'Men, along with 'older teachers, secondary teachers, *senior managers, and teachers who had worked in another profession* felt most strongly that a *high status profession* is characterised by reward and respect' (p16, original emphasis) and that teaching is not: 'those intending to leave teaching in the next five years were also strongly of this opinion'. Overall the first tranche of Teachers Status Project responses suggest that teachers view 'teaching and a high status profession ... [as being] at opposite poles' (p17). They also show that teachers perceive a significant decline in the status of teaching over the past 36 years (p18).

The Teachers Status Project interim findings concur in various ways with those of the GTC (2003), MacBeath *et al* (2004) and Mahony and Hextall (2000) in that what teachers most want is 'better understanding by the public and policy-makers', which in turn 'indicates the sense of being misunderstood and undervalued' (p21). The GTC study found that teachers feel they get little respect from the media (86%), from government (78%), or the general public (68%). The most recent survey for the GTC by NFER of over 4000 teachers found that most teachers saw the status of the profession as being 'at or below the midpoint of the five-point scale' (Sturman *et al*, 2005:11).

McBeath and Galton's (2004) survey of secondary teachers for the National Union of Teachers (NUT) found that statutory testing and the current inspection regime had the most negative effect on their work, while the National Curriculum, KS3 strategy and target setting was viewed positively by the majority of teachers. However, their main finding was that pupil behaviour had the most negative effect on teacher's lives (see also chapter 8, Getting Out). Pupil behaviour may certainly be linked by teachers to notions of respect and thus affect their status within society.

St. John-Brooks (2001:26) identifies three key elements to teachers status: pay and conditions, public attitudes and morale. Public attitudes clearly link into notions of respect and she argues that pay is not crucial but becomes so if the other two are undermined.

While media headlines and government quangos might suggest otherwise, public opinion polls generally indicate that teachers are respected and that parents are satisfied with their children's teachers (GTC, 2000). Nevertheless, a 1999 Unesco Report (cited by St. John-Brooks) found teachers in many countries complaining about low status and respect. The media, and especially some of their banner headlines, can have a significant impact on teachers' morale.

Barnard (2000:8) cites a survey of 650 NQTs which found that two-thirds thought that they were entering a profession 'which is not valued or respected by society'. One of our own respondents put it this way.

> ... if I go into teaching it's probably one of the least paid options available, whereas if you go into something marketing or advertising you can work yourself up the scale a lot faster. But I don't think pay's everything and it certainly doesn't help that the teachers have such a bad deal in the press. You know, every time you open a

newspaper you hardly hear anything good being said about the teachers, it's always like, 'Oh the teachers are on strike again', and the teachers are, you know, do this and they get a very bad press report... I think their status is low... I think rather than the government always saying teachers must do this, must do that and have to prove themselves and so on, they should occasionally praise them and say yes they are doing a good job. (Reid and Thornton, 2000:46)

Whilst parents express satisfaction at the micro and meso levels with the teachers with whom they have contact, the national media reports parental concern about teachers in general and this is what teachers read about themselves in the press. They are blamed for all kinds of things, from substance abuse and indiscipline to teenage pregnancies and the lower achievements of boys. If we look at the elements contributing to teacher status (St. John Brookes, 2001) and the initial outcomes of the Cambridge Teachers Status Project, we can see that morale is low, that public attitudes to teachers in general as a workforce, are ambivalent and thus pay becomes an issue.

Our respondents from the Men's Club (Appendix A4) believe that men generally are attracted to high status, highly paid jobs. Teaching is neither, but they do envisage rapid promotion, as men, to more highly paid positions, a factor in teaching that has been evidenced by a number of studies (Reid and Thornton, 2000; Thornton and Bricheno, 2000; Lynch 1994, Warren 1997). Ul-Haq *et al* (2003:175), working with business students confirm this male preference for career advancement. Their male respondents

> ... favoured more concrete gains such as promotion and salary increase... whereas female respondents preferred the thought of wider career opportunities and credibility in the workplace.

The issue of career advancement is addressed in chapter 7. Once teaching has been chosen as a career, perceived male advantage has not been evidenced as having a significant impact on the initial recruitment of men (Drudy *et al*, 2005; Reid and Thornton, 2000). Rather, it seems to act more as a reassurance for men who have already chosen it as an atypical career path.

If the government is serious about attracting more good quality entrants, including men, into teaching, issues relating to low status such as pay, public perceptions and morale need to be addressed. Pay alone will not raise the status of teaching as a career.

Suspicious minds: paedophiles and gays?

Public panics occur around paedophilia as they do around boys' low achievement and laddish behaviour. Francis and Skelton (2001) suggest that this may be another deterrent to men becoming teachers and it is a concern, along with child abuse, that until the 1980s was not a focus of public or media gaze. As a distinct and relatively recent concern this may well have an impact on missing men in education.

There can be no doubt that men opting for primary teaching are perceived by many people as odd. Tom (BEd Year 4) said

> I was chatting to my grandmother, about coming here (to talk to the researcher) and she said... men shouldn't be in primary classrooms. I thought thanks! ... I've also found it's a low self-esteem sort of job in some ways for men... from their point of view (and) how others view them...it's not a thing that a man should be doing.

Another student, Alistair (BEd Year 1) expressed concern lest he be considered a potential child molester and a pervert. None of this is unusual: it fits well with the homophobic nature of hegemonic masculinity. Real men don't do so-called feminine things like teaching, so men who teach can't be real men: they must be paedophiles or gays.

Hill (2005:7), reporting on men as early years childcare workers, cites Jackie Turner, a single mum who 'admits she was initially suspicious' of such an arrangement:

> I wondered why any man would choose to do it... It took me a while to get used to the idea. But now I am delighted: the children get a different sort of attention from John. He takes them out to do all sorts of energetic stuff and they come back worn out. I wasn't looking for a male role model but it's a wonderful off-shoot to the arrangement. Harry (child) loves spending time with him.

This is the classic outcome for men who choose teaching and one that many women who are lone parents seek for their sons. To protect their masculinity and offset suspicions of paedophilia and homosexuality male teachers may choose or come under pressure to accentuate their *real* man characteristics (Sargent, 2001:80).

Reasons for choosing teaching

We undertook a large scale survey, partly funded by the TTA, of *Students' Reasons for Choosing Primary Teaching as a Career* (Reid and Thornton, 2000). This research provided a description of a large number of students successfully recruited to ITE courses and identi-fied a range of reasons for their career choice. Similar studies have been undertaken by Carrington (2002), Johnston *et al* (1998, 1999) and Drudy *et al* (2005): the latter two, both based outside England and Wales, included school leavers as well as student teachers in their surveys. Our sample, the largest in terms of student teachers, was drawn from fourteen different higher education institutions in England and covered first year under-graduates and PGCE primary students. 1611 questionnaires were completed and 148 follow-up interviews conducted. The gender sample for both was very close to the current intake figures of approximately 15 per cent men and 85 per cent women.

In all these studies student teachers overwhelmingly choose teach-ing as a career for positive reasons. In our study nine out of ten of all the new students thought that the fact that they enjoyed working with children was important. More than 95 per cent felt that teach-ing would bring high job satisfaction, would be a good career and would be a challenge. These are all very positive reasons for choos-ing to teach. However, there were some gender differences in res-ponses which usefully illustrate some of the points already made and may help to explain male absence from teaching.

In accord with other research, both in and outside teaching (Ul-Haq *et al*, 2003), men appear more likely than women to be attracted by factors such as salary, status and conditions of service. Women are more likely than men to be attracted to working with children and wanting to make a genuine difference. In Johnston *et al*'s study (1998, 1999) salary ranked sixth for men, ninth for women. This was a statistically significant difference. In relation to the attractions of teaching more men than women in our study also considered long holidays to be important (34% to 24%). Whilst many studies (Thornton, 1999b; Coleman, 2002) identify rapid career advance-ment for male teachers as another feature of their career choice, Johnston *et al* (1998, 1999) found no evidence for this.

Real life experience of working with teachers in classrooms had a great impact on our students' reasons for choosing teaching as a career. For some it was positive memories of their own teachers but for most it was based on work experience in the sixth form, as parental helpers, working as educational support workers or visiting schools. This should not be surprising since work experience is likely to be a strong motivator for or against teaching as a career and is more likely to produce realistic expectations of what such work actually involves, including whether or not it is feminised. However, more women than men thought that pre-course experience in schools was an important factor in their career choice. As work experience placements are predominantly sex-typed, they are unlikely to prompt men to think about teaching.

A higher proportion of men than women in our survey come into teacher training as mature entrants or as career-changers (38% compared to 28%): Carrington's (2002) figures were similar (36% males and 27% females), showing that some men are willing to consider teaching as a career as they grow in age and maturity, or as they become dissatisfied with their current work situation. Perhaps when they have families of their own, they have acquired a more positive attitude to men working with young children and are more willing and able to cross the gender divide.

Gender differences are apparent regarding the intellectual aspect of teachers work. Although men are usually more subject-oriented than women, in our survey more women than men wanted to use their academic knowledge and to continue their studies (77% and 70% of women compared with 66% and 51% of men).

Choosing teaching because the hours fit in better with parenting is seen as more important by women than by men (41% to 17%), although this figure represents a minority of women respondents and could be linked to concerns about career interruption for having children. Women are more likely than men to see teaching as a good fall-back career (26% and 17% respectively).

Supporting Drudy *et al*'s (2005) findings in Ireland, our student teachers differentiate between primary and secondary teaching as a career. More men than women thought that the secondary school age group was less disciplined (56% compared to 26%), and that the National Curriculum was too rigid at this level (32% to 13%). However, more women than men lacked confidence in teaching this age group (48% and 35%). Contrary to Johnston *et al* (1998, 1999), Drudy *et al*'s respondents, both male and female, thought that secondary teaching had lower status than primary teaching but they also had more stereotypical views of primary teaching as women's work and this was considerably more the case for boys than for girls, who were more likely to see primary teaching as suitable for both.

To summarise, men student teachers are more likely than women to attach greater importance to longer holidays, career change and having few other job opportunities than women, whereas women student teachers are more likely to attach greater importance to entering a career that fits better with parenthood. In all these studies, the overwhelming majority of both men and women enter teaching for intrinsic and altruistic reasons rather than for extrinsic ones. There are not many male recruits but those there are generally want to work with children and see it as a challenging, rewarding and worthwhile occupation.

The most common explanation given by student teachers for the absence of men, especially in primary teaching, is that it is perceived to be women's work (Johnston *et al*, 1998, 1999: Drudy *et al*, 2005; Carrington, 2002).

> Still seen as a ladies' job, primary teaching, should be more of a profession like secondary teaching. You are a professional but people do not see you as one. (Reid and Thornton, 2000: 25)

However, both male and female student teachers do perceive teaching to be a career in which men are needed, and see that their contribution is valuable. For some this is expressed as a counterbalance to its feminisation and the inevitable assumption that boys need male teachers as role models. Some powerful arguments have already been put forward against seeing teachers as role models. Nevertheless, the physical presence of men in schools, indicating that teaching is a suitable job for men as well as for women, might at least prompt boys to consider teaching as a possible career.

Unlike Drudy *et al* (2005), who emphasise the centrality of care as a core social value that should be as relevant to men as it is women, and whose adoption by society in general is necessary for more men to be recruited to teaching, we suggest, with Ashley and Lee (2003), that a more professional and gender-neutral conception of teaching should be developed, where wanting to work with children and caring about their educational development, rather than caring for them in a parental sense, is the key to teacher recruitment, making teaching an attractive career option for all who care about children's learning, including many men.

At a pragmatic level, what can be done to increase male and female recruitment to teaching? Our recommendations to the TTA included the following:

- ■ Non-traditional work-experience placements to widen the career options considered by men and women, because the chances of them choosing an atypical career that they have little knowledge or experience of are small.

- Target male and female career-changers and mature entrants.

- Place greater emphasis on the status, salary, working conditions and career opportunities available in teaching.

- Challenge the image of teaching as a relatively low-status, feminised occupation through sustained positive publicity that emphasises the value of all teachers to society, the real rather than the assumed content and activities it involves, the challenge, responsibility, rewards and job satisfaction that teaching can bring, and its cross-gender appropriateness.

These are really short-term strategies with much wider implications for how gender and education are perceived in our society. Education is caring about and working with children but despite perceptions it is not feminised: if anything it is increasingly masculinised in terms of structures, roles, activity and content (Mahony *et al*, 2004b; Arnot *et al*, 1999). Major deterrents for the recruitment of more men are: the widespread belief that it is feminised, women's work and that men who do it might be paedophile or gay, plus societal prejudice and peer group pressure on men to be *real* men and not to deviate from hegemonic forms of masculinity that place care about and work with children firmly in the female domain. Teaching needs to be recast as a high status job because of what it involves, not because to do so might attract more men. And this implies the removal of misogynist and patriarchal structures that allocate occupational status on the basis of gender.

Trap door entrants

Is teaching, as so notably described by Willard Waller (1965) in his seminal 1932 book, *The Sociology of Teaching,* 'the refuge of unsaleable men and unmarriageable women'? We would argue not, though the incidence of men entering teaching by chance rather than choice is clearly documented, and the marriage bar actually required that women teachers remained single. Waller's statement matches that of the 1925 Board of Education who claimed that men 'would not do it if fit for anything else' (Oram, 1989:22), and that of George Bernard Shaw (1903) who famously said 'He who can, does. He who cannot, teaches'.

Such statements suggest lack of commitment to teaching and that it is not a job worth doing by those who have realistic alternatives. This is a serious part of the problem regarding recruitment to teaching and at least some of the blame lies with the Careers Service!

Citing an Australian proposal to positively discriminate in favour of men by offering them scholarships to train as teachers, Mills (2005:13) stresses that the negative outcome would be for men to be viewed as less committed than women to teaching.

Studies of male teachers have consistently found gender differences in teacher recruitment. Scott *et al* (1998) note that only 37 per cent of men in their sample had always wanted to teach (as opposed to 50% of women); 48 per cent had not made teaching their first career choice (compared with 38% of women), and 23 per cent were teaching because they lacked alternative career options, but this applied to only 16 per cent of women. Poll (cited Mancus, 1992:111) found that teaching was usually a compromise career option for men and in Skelton's (1991) sample of eleven male early years teachers, only two 'had always wanted to teach'. The work of Williams and Villemez (1993), Jacobs (1993), Brookhart and Loadman, (1996) and others, on atypical occupational choices in America, support the findings of the English researchers and our own research, which are that more men are to be found in stereotypically female occupations than actually aspire to them, with more men than women entering teaching through a trap door effect of availability or convenience rather than through positive choice.

Although our survey (Reid and Thornton, 2000) found that almost all the students chose teaching because they wanted to teach, more men than women had done another job and wanted a change (41% to 30%), and more men than women said that they had few other job opportunities (12% to 5%). In our student teacher interviews 43 per cent of men made negative comments about their previous work experiences outside education. Their concerns were focused on things like being in the wrong job, being bored with it and seeing it as a dead-end in terms of a career. Only 21 per cent of women interviewees said similar things. These men said they had 'drifted into A levels and industry, were not mature enough for teaching'; 'had a variety of other jobs and wanted something different'; had 'worked in various dead end jobs', and 'believed I could offer something of myself to this job and I also believed I [as a man] was needed'.

In addition, some of the students in our Men's Club (Thornton, 1999b), rather than those who were career changers, came into teaching because they failed to get the grades necessary for their first choice university course. This doesn't necessarily mean that men are less committed to teaching, even though it may not be the first choice career for all. Recent research (Parry, 2005:13) suggests that once trap door entrants are teaching their commitment to teaching as a career is strong, there are no obvious differences in teacher quality and even that they are more likely to stay in teaching, demonstrating greater, not less, commitment to teaching as a career.

A more viable explanation for the later arrival of some men in teaching is that with age, maturity and perhaps children of their own, a stronger sense of the individualised self emerges, and it becomes easier to go against the disapproval of former adolescent peers and to choose an atypical career. There is also some evidence of disillusionment with earlier choices of typically male careers, as not being sufficiently challenging or rewarding. It is then possible that potential male teachers need more time and experience to identify what really interests them, rather than conforming to what school peers and significant others suggest hegemonic masculinity prescribes for them.

Hill (2005:7) quotes Mark Shepherd, a 36 year old Black childminder.

> An increasing number of wives are earning more than their husbands, so men are staying at home to bring up the children. Once they have that experience they realise that, despite what society has told them about men not being able to look after children, they can do it and do it well. Five years ago, no parents would have trusted me to look after their children but now my business is thriving. It's my perfect job.

Dean (2001:12) cites Richard, a failed chef who now manages a nursery.

> ...parents like the idea of a male child-carer ... our greatest challenge is to win their trust... more important for children to have a positive and reliable male role model in their lives... childcare is a highly challenging career, whether you are a man or a woman... but it is very rewarding.

Conclusions

We agree with Mills (2005:15) that

> For more men to be encouraged into the teaching profession, the homophobia and misogyny that are responsible for the current gendered construction of primary teaching have to be challenged.

This runs counter to the view that macho male teachers are needed to bond with boys and to role model hegemonic masculinity. What education needs are alternative examples of masculinity. That some men can and do cross these barriers for good educational reasons rather than financial or status incentives, even if some do it later than others, is a step in the right direction.

Recommended reading

Chris Skelton presents a strong case for not viewing teaching as 'feminised' in Skelton, C. (2002) The 'feminisation of schooling' or 're-masculinising' primary education, *International Studies in the Sociology of Education*, 12 (1), pp77-96.

Sheelagh Drudy and colleagues provide a thorough account of gendered perceptions of teaching as a career in Drudy, S., Martin, M., Woods, M. and O'Flynn, J. (2005) *Men and the Classroom: gender imbalances in teaching*, London: RoutledgeFalmer.

5
Getting In

Introduction

The fact that many men choose not to consider teaching as a career is of key concern but what happens when they do decide that teaching is for them? We have already demonstrated a greater tendency amongst men than women to work with older children, to highlight career advancement and financial incentives, and academic rather than care or nurturing-type reasons for teaching. This is demonstrated in several ways in terms of getting men into teacher training and their selected entry routes and age-phases.

Since its inception the TDA has proved itself successful in increasing student teacher numbers and teacher supply across all phases and subjects with some smaller scale impact on male and ethnic minority recruitment. This was achieved by high-profile advertising campaigns, many aimed directly at men and ethnic minorities and by the diversification of routes into teaching. At the same time the TDA received substantial government support in the form of funding for training salaries, increases in teachers pay and workload reform. Teaching has become a better paid and relatively more attractive career, so that in 2005 we are on the verge of over-supply in the primary sector. Vacancies in primary schools have declined from 2,110 in January 2001 to 740 in January 2005 and some schools are reporting up to 100 applicants for every job (Bloom, 2005). Unfortunately headships do not attract similar numbers of applicants.

The Government's case to the 2005 teacher's pay review body suggests a 2 per cent pay rise this year, on the basis that

Teachers' pay now compares favourably relative to all other non-manual and graduate workers, except in London and the South-east. The real terms improvements... over recent years... structural changes, and the improvements ... to job quality through workload reform, have improved the competitiveness of the teaching profession with other graduate professions. (cited Stewart and Lucas, 2005c:3)

Perhaps surprisingly, pay review evidence from the teacher's professional associations says something similar,

... that average classroom teacher pay had increased by 15 per cent above inflation since 1997 and pay was 'no longer the key priority' in seeking to improve teacher recruitment and retention. (cited Stewart and Lucas, 2005c:3)

Primary teacher training places will now be gradually cut back to reduce over-supply and this is likely to increase competition for places available. The situation in secondary training is somewhat different, with teacher supply varying more by subject. However, increased competition for training places is unlikely to increase the number of men entering teaching, as shown below.

Qualifications, entry criteria and interviews

The establishment of the TTA in 1994 and the subsequent range of government initiatives to improve the attractiveness of teaching as a career, as well as the quality of teachers, had their origins in 1990s concerns about inadequate supply and retention of good quality teachers. In 1997 the average 'A' level points score for new students was 13.6 (House of Commons, 1997:1), considerably lower than what was required for most other undergraduate courses. Nickell and Quintini (2002) suggest that men entering teaching in the early 1990s were less able than their predecessors in the previous generation (1970s) and sought to demonstrate this by comparing each of these generations' test results at age ten years.

Our own research confirms the relatively low entry points of undergraduate primary trainees. The average entry point score was 12.5; for the group of men it was 11.6 and for the matched group of women it was 13.3. In both our Matched Cohort Longitudinal study (2003, Appendix A8) and our Men's Club case study (1999a and Appendix A4) we found men's average 'A' Level point scores to be lower than women's, despite being on the same course at the same institution. Attempts to match male and female students exactly in terms of age, entry criteria and subject specialism were not always possible. It was also difficult to find female students, who matched in other respects, with 'A' level points scores as low as those of the men.

Whilst entry qualifications are now rising, particularly for post-graduate trainees (PG), concerns still remain about student teacher entry levels relative to other undergraduate (UG) and PG courses and careers. As we shall see below, the total package of routes into teaching now available seem to emphasise PG entry (preferably with a 2.1 classification or above). The new routes also tend to target highly qualified recruits, particularly through paid PG work-based training: there has been a dramatic increase in PG trainee numbers alongside stagnating UG numbers. UG numbers in ITT were 8,100 in 2000 and 8,180 in 2004, whereas PG numbers in ITT were 19,620 in 2000 but 25,840 in 2004 (DfES, 2004). Given that men have been found more critical than women of university-based courses (Brookhart and Loadman, 1996:208)) and more responsive to finan-cial incentives – male enquiries increased by 18 per cent when train-ing salaries were introduced (Barnard, 2000:8) – this policy could eventually succeed in increasing the numbers of male recruits to teaching but must be set against the relatively lower entry qualifica-tions of male applicants. If competition for training places continues to increase, women should be better positioned to get them.

Why is it that men who get into teacher training are more likely to have lower entry qualifications than women? In the past when single sex colleges and training courses were more common, it was pos-sible for parallel men's and women's colleges to accept different minimum entrance standards – much like single sex grammar schools of old – based on supply and demand considerations e.g. the top 10 per cent of applicants to each college get places regardless of the actual level of qualification. Johnston *et al* (1998, 1999) point to such practices in Northern Ireland, prior to the integration of single-sex colleges into co-ed ones and despite requiring much higher entrance points overall than colleges in England. Integration in Northern Ireland teacher education has led to a convergence of men's and women's entry qualifications at an almost identical level of 22 points now and competition for places remains strong. Whether or not this has effectively reduced the numbers of male entrants is unclear, as gender proportions have fluctuated much more in Northern Ireland than in the UK.

The focus on recruiting more men, especially to primary teaching, and the allocation of targets by the TDA to training providers has the propensity to encourage admissions tutors to favour male applicants. In discussing the increasing proportions of women entering higher education in general, and concerns expressed in some quarters about this, Louis Hirsch, admissions director at the University of Delaware says,

> ... gender comes into play at the margins. When you look at applications that could go either way, if the applicant is male that may be a reason for tilting to the side of 'yes'. Phillips (2005:20-21)

Does concern for missing men in education weigh the odds in favour of affirmative action? Officially it does not: entry requirements at undergraduate (primary) level are a minimum of two 'A' levels; English, Maths and Science GCSE at grade C; two weeks continuous experience in school, plus an interview, a self-declaration of fitness to teach (physical and mental) and a criminal records check. For PGCE secondary a good first degree is also required but not GCSE Science, and for work-based routes, primary or secondary, very similar qualifications. Initial offers of places are based on these general criteria plus interviews.

Interviews and selection criteria

Student teacher selection criteria are an under-researched area. The literature says very little about this although there have been indications that disproportionately more men than women are rejected by admissions tutors (Gates, 1999). This may simply be due to lower qualification at the point of application, especially for over-subscribed courses such as the primary PGCE and some secondary school subjects (e.g. PE and History). At the next stage of getting into teaching, the interview, men may be in a stronger position to sell themselves. Interviews are required to assess a general 'suitability for teaching' with particular reference to experience with young people, commitment to teaching and the possession of relevant knowledge and skills. They may also involve applicants in group discussion, teaching a mini-lesson or giving a presentation (TTA, 2005).

Little attention has been given to the relationship between interview assessments and student drop-out but it has been suggested that for secondary PGCE students such interviews may not explore a candidate's motivations for teaching and their awareness of the reality of teaching in sufficient depth (Chambers and Roper, 2000). When we explored selection criteria in our Matched Cohort Longitudinal study (Appendix A8), we found some gender differences in interview assessments that later correlated with persistence/failure/drop-out rates (see chapter 6). More men than women students who had relatively low interview assessments had been accepted onto this particular BEd course, raising concerns about how the selection criteria had been applied. We found that criteria such as academic qualifications and age are relatively reliable predictors of successful completion, whereas interview assessments are not.

Hooton's (1997) study of the Diploma in Social Work in Scotland found that selection criteria relating to student motivation was the most effective predictor of both academic and practice achievement. Academic background and previous social work experiences were found to be partial indicators of success. But there was no correlation between the selection process and the outcome of the course. This research is mentioned since it has some features in common with the teaching degree: the gender balance on the courses i.e. 70.5 per cent female and 29.5 per cent male, the vocational, motivational requirements of the subject and the selection process (academic qualifications and interviews to assess suitability for training).

Are admissions tutors for teacher training engaging in some sort of affirmative action here? Is it appropriate, for the sake of a better gender balance to accept male students with lower entry qualifications or interview assessments? We know, from substantial experience within the field, that some male students, presenting as immature and unfocused at eighteen or nineteenth, can grow and develop into committed, dedicated and able teachers, although some of them do not (Smedley, 1997; Foster and Newman, 2001a). Should more risks be taken when considering male applicants, perhaps because there are relatively so few of them? A key theme of this book is that what we most need in education are high quality committed teachers. If this can be achieved together with a more representative teaching force, so much the better. However, teacher gender should not be the prime consideration in terms of entrance qualifications: potential teacher quality should be. With penalties for poor retention co-existing alongside rewards for meeting gender targets, it is a tough decision for training providers but decisions about entry should be based on equal merit and potential for success, not the gender – or ethnicity – of the applicant.

Different training routes

The undergraduate training courses, all based in higher education institutions, have predominantly prepared teachers for primary schools. The PGCE, again HE-based, has been the traditional route into secondary teaching but also supplies increasing numbers of primary teachers, attracted by the bursaries attached to this route which were originally called training salaries, and until this year, the wavering of top-up fees for PGCE students. Similar financial benefits have not been attached to the undergraduate entry routes and some commentators have suggested that this further devalues primary teachers and teaching (Gates, 1999).

There are now abundant financial incentives to train to teach, a factor which according to research evidence should encourage more men into training, despite the general increase in costs to individual students of a higher education in England. The introduction of £6,000 bursaries in 2000 resulted in a 5 per cent increase in male applicants, and an 18 per cent increase in male enquiries (TTA figures cited Barnard, 2000:8). From 2006 all PGCE students, both primary and secondary, will be liable for up to £3,000 top-up fees but alongside this they will get a bursary of at least £6,000, plus a non-means tested LEA grant of £1,200 and means-tested support of up to £1,500 from the government. Maths and Science PGCEs will get an additional £3,000 added to their bursaries and 'golden hellos' of £5,000 when they complete their teaching induction year. Other shortage subjects (RE, Music, Modern Languages, ICT, Design and Technology, English and Drama) will get the same £9,000 bursaries but a smaller 'golden hello' of £2,500. With recent increases in salary the financial incentives are good.

New routes into teaching also have financial incentives attached to them. The *Teaching Taster* (TT) route enables students to earn credits towards QTS whilst at the same time completing their first degree. It encourages them to consider a subsequent teaching career and it should shorten their training period but there are problems in terms of how UG training credits can actually be offset against a PGCE course. So far the indications are that students in-volved in TT were already considering teaching as a career.

The *Flexi-PGCE* is HE-based, allows for part-time study over five terms and when first introduced by the Open University also came with a free lap-top. Like the work-based routes outlined below, the flexi-PGCE allows students to earn salaries whilst also studying to become teachers, a key issue for career changers and mature en-trants. As we have seen in chapter 4, men are more likely than women to enter teaching as career-changers, although both enter in significant numbers as mature students.

School Centred Initial Teacher Training (SCITT) routes are primarily run by schools for post-graduate trainees rather than by HE providers. SCITTs were recognised by some of our TTA respondents (Appendix A6) as a possible and different route into teaching but they also suggested that it was not a particularly good route to take. Its status may be affected by Ofsted reports of the relatively poor performance of SCITT providers.

The *Graduate Teacher Programme (GTP)* and the *Registered Teacher Programme (RTP)* are work-based training routes. GTP students already have a degree and usually complete their training in one year. RTP students have the equivalent of two years degree level study on entry and complete their degree whilst training, which usually takes two years. Both routes pay unqualified teacher salaries during training.

The *Teach First* programme gives graduates a taste of classroom life by working in disadvantaged London schools and has proved a successful initiative with half of participants remaining in teaching following their work experience. Based on the *Teach for America* programme, it pays schools £2000 for each trainee and encourages graduates 'who would never think about teaching to go into it for two years' (Parry, 2005:13). There was a 90 per cent completion rate in its first two years, and all of these students obtained QTS. *Teach First* pays slightly less than an NQT gets in the first year and at NQT rates plus London weighting in the second year. Students attend residential summer schools in HE, receive mentoring and work 80 per cent of the timetable. In the USA around 40 per cent stay in teaching and another 20 per cent within education. The UK scheme began in 2003 and has succeeded in attracting some very able applicants.

The TDA plans to double the number of work-based trainees by 2006, to 20 per cent of all student teachers, despite considerably higher costs than for traditional HE-based training. It must also be noted that Ofsted reports suggest that work and school-based training provides a 'narrow experience of teaching', with more unsatisfactory lessons observed during inspections: one in five, as opposed to one in 10. However, they appear to attract good candidates and have good completion rates with nine out of ten obtaining QTS (Ofsted, 2005c)

There is one additional, soon to be ended, new route into teaching, called *Fast Track (FT)* (DfEE, 1998). It requires candidates to have good entry qualifications ('A' levels at 22 points minimum, and a 2.1

degree or above), ambition, a strong commitment to driving change, and the potential to be an excellent leader. It provides a training bursary of £5,000 plus a free lap-top. Fast Track NQTs start one point higher than other NQTs on the pay scale and they receive additional training to speed them into management positions. In return there are no limits on FT trainees' working time. The number of men students applying to FT, and acquiring places on this route, are disproportionate to the numbers of men entering teaching by other routes.

In 2003 (Thornton, 2003:12) there were 88 NQT arriving through FT, 22 experienced FT teachers (in their first five years) and 117 in training, at a cost of £14 million. FT costs around £35,000 per recruit, which is very expensive compared to other routes. On average there have been around 350 recruits a year, not the 1,000 expected. From 2006 FT will be re-focused as a leadership development programme for qualified teachers and will no longer recruit trainees.

Variations by route and gender

The *Becoming a Teacher Project* (Malderez *et al*, 2004: 15-17) has explored variations in route, gender and age-phase amongst teacher education students in an on-going longitudinal study (2003-2009). Their initial findings suggest that:

- Undergraduates are more likely than PGCE students to say that they want to work with children or young people (68% as opposed to 50%) whereas PGCE students are more likely than undergraduates to say they want to stay involved with their subject (36% as opposed 16% or less) and are concerned about career development (25% as opposed 12%).

- Flexi and RTP/GTP students are more likely than undergraduates to want to 'give something back' (41% as opposed to 24% or less).

- Primary students are more likely than secondary students to say they want to work with children or young people (73% as opposed to 45%), that helping youngsters to learn is important to them (82% as opposed to 75%), and they are less likely to be attracted by available career opportunities (15% as opposed to 23%) or staying involved with their subject (15% as opposed to 42%).

- Women students are more likely than men students to say they want to work with children or young people (66% as opposed to 38%) and that helping youngsters to learn is important to them (81% as opposed to 69%), whereas men students cited financial incentives and the benefits packages (e.g. occupational pension) more than women (52% as opposed to 38% and 36% as opposed to 26% respectively).

There are some familiar gender and age-phase patterns here. Working with children and young people is more typical of primary teachers, who are disproportionately women and who disproportionately train to teach through undergraduate study. Secondary teachers are more concerned with the subjects they teach and the greater career opportunities available to them. Men are more focused than women on financial rewards. Yet the differences, whilst noticeable, are not huge in percentage terms. The largest difference refers to work with children and young people: a gap of 28 per cent between men and women. This is offset by the high percentages of primary (82%), secondary (75%), men (69%) and women (81%) saying that helping young people to learn is important to them. While the phrase 'working with children and young people' may be a lesser choice for subject-oriented secondary teachers and men protective of their masculine identities, clearly 'helping young people to learn' is not. Perhaps this is the proper focus for all intending teachers and it is refreshing to see that it is so firmly stated in this research. It emphasises the professional teacher's *care about* role.

Age-phase variation

Anecdotal evidence suggests that in the past some men entering teacher training have been channelled into training to teach older children if a primary course, or secondary if a cross-phase course, by both male and female lecturers. Men are assumed to be better suited to teaching older children whatever the age-phase and more interested in subject specialisms. This is not just a gender issue as some female students who are considered to be more able academically are also encouraged to train to teach older children, perhaps being advised that they are wasting their talents by training to teach younger children. The gender pressure conforms to hegemonic definitions of masculinity and the ability pressure to, often male, beliefs that teaching younger children is easier and of lower status.

It is difficult to assess how prevalent such views are today, although evidence from our TTA survey (Reid and Thornton, 2000) suggests that some teachers and careers advisers persist in perpetuating this kind of advice. Certainly more men apply for secondary and upper primary training than do for lower primary and early years. Some of our Men's Club respondents (Appendix A4) confirm a preference for upper primary based on 'more academically challenging work'.

> I know a friend... he really struggled when he went home. His friends ribbed him about it, him being a primary school teacher ... It wasn't mentally challenging enough for a male. (Thom, Men's Club)

By way of contrast some men students favour lower primary/early years (aged 3 to 7) because they anticipate more discipline problems in upper primary (aged 7 to 11). As another Men's Club student, Alan notes, 'younger children are a little bit easier to control aren't they!'

It is possible that some male students cite academic work with older children as a counter to views expressed by families and friends that stigmatise primary teaching as a career for men. As Skelton notes, the younger the child the lower the status of its teacher (1991:280).

Conclusions

The plethora of routes into teaching has evolved in response to teacher shortages and the government initiative to raise entry standards, whilst at the same time widening the pool of potential recruits to include more men and ethnic minority teachers alongside career changers, mature entrants and others for whom the traditional routes were either inaccessible or unattractive. They appear to be succeeding in general supply terms. According to the TDA Annual Report (2005) the number of trainees has increased with over 42000 beginning courses in September 2005, the highest number since 1975; employment-based training routes accounted for nearly 17 per cent of those in training. In 2004, the percentage of trainees from minority ethnic groups rose from 8.8 per cent to 9.4 per cent. However, the number of men training to be primary teachers showed little improvement.

In England, the proportion of men training to teach has consistently declined over the past twenty years (see chapter 3): this could be linked to Government and TDA efforts to raise entry requirements, and a narrowing of the gap between men's and women's entry qualifications.

Some concerns remain regarding how entry criteria are used, especially interview assessments, which try to assess personal suitability and which are inevitably more subjective: this requires some serious in-depth study. Interview assessments used for appointments and promotions in teaching have certainly been questioned in terms of gender bias (see chapter 7).

At the same time, the financial incentives, more frequently cited by men than women as important in getting into teaching, have attracted more inquiries about training and is bringing better qualified men and women into teaching. Getting into teaching isn't easy, but what happens to men when they are accepted onto teacher training courses? The experiences of men in training are examined in chapter 6.

Recommended reading

Ofsted Reports on different entry routes to teaching such as: Ofsted (2002), The Graduate Teacher Programme (HMI 346, January 2002), The Stationery Office, London; Flexible postgraduate initial teacher training (Ofsted, 2003a); An evaluation of the Training Schools programme (Ofsted, 2003b); An employment-based route into teaching: An overview of the first year of the inspection of designated recommended bodies for the Graduate Teacher Programme 2003/04 (Ofsted, 2005c), can be found at www.ofsted.gov.uk

For current guidance on entry routes into teaching visit the TDA web site at http://www.tda.gov.uk/Recruit/thetrainingprocess/typesofcourse.aspx

6
Getting Through

Introduction

Teacher supply has certainly improved, and there has been some progress in recruiting more men to teacher training. However, once on a training course, men are more likely to go missing than their women peers: they are more likely to fail, drop-out or transfer to alternative HE courses. In this chapter we explore the patterns of male drop-out from both quantitative and qualitative perspectives, illuminating men's experience of teacher training, and possible reasons for them not successfully completing their training as teachers.

Some of the patterns we identify apply across HE, others just to teaching, across all age-phases. However, to highlight some of the key issues and patterns affecting men training to teach we will also focus indepth on studies of men training to be primary or early years teachers through traditional HE routes, namely the primary BEd and the PGCE. These trainees are most at odds with hegemonic definitions of suitable careers for men, have the least financial incentive for training to teach, and may, because of their career choice, be under the greatest gender pressure, both within and outside the profession. By focusing on primary and early years teaching we illustrate, through the words of male trainees, some of the issues which impact upon their formal and informal education as teachers.

Who gets through?

There are numerous small-scale studies of men training to teach in primary schools (Skelton and Hanson, 1989; Allen, 1994; Foster,

1995; Emery, 1997; Smedley, 1997; Thornton, 2000a; Foster and New-man, 2001b; Lewis 2002). Many report the difficulties for men in successfully completing these courses. Higher failure and non-completion rates are commonly reported as is disproportionate over-representation in the lower classes of the degree classification system.

Our early study (Thornton, 1999a; Appendix A2) also found that male education students fail in disproportionate numbers to complete their training successfully. As illustrated in Table 1 opposite, non-completion for men on the primary PGCE ranged from 27 per cent at its lowest to 31 per cent at its highest over two cohorts. For men on the BEd non-completion ranged from 33 per cent to 56 per cent over three cohorts. For women the highest non-completion rate over both courses and cohorts was 18 per cent. The withdrawal and failure rates on the primary PGCE were generally lower than for undergraduate trainees but still appreciably different for men and women students.

Although the figures in Table 1 relate to one institution, these patterns are confirmed elsewhere. Foster (1995) found non-completion rates of up to 66 per cent for men on PGCE primary courses; Furedi (2000) reports that men are twice as likely to drop out of their primary PGCE course than women, and Moyles and Cavendish, (2001) found that three times more men than women had to retake failed coursework or teaching placements. Variations in degree classification have also been found (Thornton, 1999a). Getting through teacher training clearly poses additional challenges for men.

Matched samples and comparisons

Our Matched Longitudinal Cohort Study (Appendix A8a) included all the 42 men studying an undergraduate degree course in Primary Education, between 1995 and 1999, plus 42 women peers matched for age, subjects studied and 'A' level points scored. We found that, for this group of students continuation into the fourth year of study was significantly related to gender and to 'A' Level point category (Chi squared tests, $p<0.05$). Women were more likely than men to complete the course successfully and there was a trend for fewer drop-outs among students with higher 'A' level points. This corresponds with the findings of other studies (Johnes and Taylor, 1989; Johnes, 1990; Woodley et al, 1992; Rickinson and Rutherford, 1995; Yorke, 1999; Martinez and Munday, 1998; Tinto, 1993).

Table 1 BEd and PGCE primary cohorts, 1992 to 1996

	Men (n)	Male %loss	Women (n)	Female %loss
1992-96 BEd				
Year 1 total 131	9		122	
Year 4 total 116	6	33% (3)	110	10% (12)
Year 4 fails	1	44% (4)	0	
1991-95 BEd				
Year 1 total 150	18		132	
Year 4 total 119	9	50% (9)	110	17% (22)
Year 4 failure	1	56% (10)	0	
1990-94 BEd				
Year 1 total 108	8		100	
Year 4 total 99	5	37% (3)	94	6% (6)
Year 4 failure	1	50% (4)	0	
1994-5 PGCE				
total 69	13		56	
Failed or withdrew	4	31% (4)	10	18% (10)
1993-4 PGCE				
total 92	11		81	
Failed or withdrew	3	27% (3)	5	6% (5)

At the end of the first year and the start of the second year of study there was a marked difference in drop-out between men and women; this was statistically significant (0.02). It is well established that the greatest drop-out occurs at the end of the first year of any programme (Tinto, 1993) but it is important to note that in this study men, especially those with lower entry qualifications, were much more likely than women to drop-out at this point.

When progress over the whole course was considered, the evidence again showed differences between men and women. Proportionately more men than women had problems with teaching placements, although some overcome these. Men also suffered more academic problems than women: 19 per cent of all men but only 11 per cent of all women struggled with these problems.

Reasons for drop-out, as recorded on student files, point to specific differences between men and women. Men much more than women make the wrong choice of course and experience academic problems. Health and finance, although causing problems for a few, are not major influences on overall drop-out.

Male numbers in studies of trainee teachers are small but although there are large-scale quantitative studies of HE drop-out, including larger numbers of men, they do not adequately deal with the specifics of education students and their programmes. To address this defect, we compared all our primary BEd students with three other programmes within the same institution (Appendix A8b).

Table 2 below, shows the number of students enrolled in each of the four programmes. The numbers of men and women enrolled on the Business Studies programme are very similar. However, there are far more men than women on Aerospace Engineering and Computer Science programmes and far more women than men on the Education programme. The numbers enrolled on the Computer Science and Education programmes are comparable.

Table 2: Numbers of male and female students enrolled on each programme in each of the cohort years

Cohort year Programme		1996 n	1997 n	1998 n
Business studies	Male	221	40	73
	Female	143	47	55
Aerospace engineer	Male	50	55	51
	Female	2	5	5
Computer science	Male	141	168	146
	Female	16	15	17
Education	Male	13	7	13
	Female	111	125	119

Chi squared tests were performed for student drop-out by gender, by age and by programme of study. These suggest that age and programme may have a significant effect on drop-out in all three years of study. Business Studies students are most likely to drop out, Education students least likely to. This is supported by earlier research (DES, 1992; Woodley *et al*, 1992; Yorke, 1999). Younger students are less likely to drop out than older students, as suggested by the DES (1992). As indicated by other researchers, men are more likely to drop-out than women, and most students are lost near the beginning of their programme (Bourner *et al*, 1991; MacDonald, 1992; Woodley *et al*, 1992; Benn, 1995; Moyles and Cavendish, 2001). The students in our comparative study are therefore shown to be similar to those observed elsewhere.

The Computer Science and Education programmes have comparable numbers of students and the observed gender differences are in opposing directions. More women drop out of Computer Science and more men drop out of the BEd (Table 3).

Table 3: Percentages for total drop out from four programmes by gender

	Male %	Female %
Aerospace engineer	37.3	45.5
Business studies	30.6	26.1
Computer science	28.8	35.9
Education	32.1	16.2

This suggests that at least some drop-out may be associated with students who are in a small minority: this is consistent with Tinto's theory that social integration in HE is more difficult for minority students (1993:62). Primary and early years' teacher training may be an extreme example of this.

Reasons given by students for leaving their programmes were varied. For Business Studies, with its comparable numbers of male and female students, the spread of reasons for leaving was also comparable. In the predominantly male domain of Computer Science almost 70 per cent gave academic problems as their reason. In the predominantly female domain of Education there were other reasons. This is supported by Yorke (1999) who found that academic difficulty was *less* likely to be a cause of drop-out for Education than for Science-based subjects, that more than in any other programme the needs of their dependents had been influential in the withdrawal of Education students, and that this was probably related to their age on entry. There is no indication that financial problems are a major cause of drop-out in our data, something confirmed by Chambers and Roper (2000), in a study of secondary PGCE students.

The categories *other* and *unknown*, comprise a large proportion of reasons for students leaving Education (61% of males and 59% of females) but categorising them as such on student records does not reveal what they are. They relate to a number of reasons which students dropping out do not wish to declare: the only way to access them is through qualitative in-depth study.

Patterns in the data

In the first of our qualitative studies (Thornton, 1999a, Appendix A2) we surveyed men BEd students at the end of their first year and those completing their fourth year, through open-ended questionnaires with an invitation to talk further through a follow-up interview. This was followed by our Men's Club case study (Thornton, 1999b, Appendix A4). Our interviews and field notes focus mainly on the men's public and professional lives. Their personal and private stories clearly inform the views they express and some of this emerged in interview, but was not directly sought.

Taken together, these studies produce a wealth of rich data over a number of years which contribute significantly to our understanding of the views of men training to be early years and primary teachers. What becomes clear is that there are substantial differences between men training to teach, as well as similarities. They are clearly not a homogeneous group with identical experiences, dispositions or responses to training to teach: it is important to remember this when seeking solutions to their poor completion rates. They vary as individuals and by categories of grouping, such as age, social class, entry qualifications and stage in training. No doubt they also vary by ethnicity, religion and culture: these areas were not explored. Nevertheless, bearing these caveats in mind, several key themes and distinct patterns emerge, in relation to successfully getting through teacher training.

Patterns relating to entry qualifications, students' age and maturity, age-range, pre-course experience and reasons for career choice and the likelihood of male students experiencing problems, such as referral or failure, during their ITE course are identifiable. There are also many helpful insights into how men training to teach primary and early years experience the professional context in which they work and how the perceptions of others affect them. These patterns and insights are illuminated by the views of the men themselves. Through our qualitative studies (Appendix A3 and A4) we have explored completion and drop-out and the kind of hindrances and drawbacks they experience.

Entry qualification, age and maturity

As indicated by statistical data, there is a tendency for men with higher entry qualifications to experience fewer problems during training than their less well qualified peers. In our Men's Club data set (Thornton, 1999b, Appendix A4) 46 per cent of students with higher entry qualifications experience problems compared to 69 per cent of those with lower qualifications. However, maturity and commitment also matter as well: overall we find that young, lower qualified direct entrants from school are more likely to experience problems during their training (83%) than young students with higher qualifications (50%), mature students with lower qualifications (60%), or mature students with higher qualifications (40%). Young men specialising in early years teaching are particularly at risk, with all these students experiencing problems, compared with half the mature early year's students. On this basis mature men with higher qualifications are most likely to succeed.

As discussed in chapters 4 and 5, maturity may be a factor in choosing teaching as a career and in gaining entrance to ITT courses: the data also suggest that maturity favours successful completion (Emery, 1997; Thornton, 1999b). Post-graduate students are usually older than undergraduates, they certainly have more extensive educational experience and possibly have a firmer commitment to primary and early years teaching. In addition, their academic ability has already been tested through their under-graduate studies.

Many of our students use the term *maturity* to explain their experiences and perceptions of primary teaching. Mature men (aged 21 and over at the start of their course) find family commitments make it more difficult to get through their training: late timetabling affects child-care and they need to spend time with their families whilst at the same time working hard for their degrees. They recognise that these problems are shared by mature women students. On the positive side, they feel that their maturity enables them to get on well with the female majority; that they are more outgoing and confident than younger men might be; they are clear about the reasons for their studies as an overt career choice and are committed to primary teaching. They also appear to be well organised in terms of getting assignments completed in good time and they claim to work hard.

Age at entry is just one variable. Of itself it is not indicative of mature attitudes, choices, behaviour or ability to access support networks. Other criteria for maturity emerge, such as a live-in partner, a child or children, or broader than average pre-course experience. One young student, Liam, has past work experience, a live-in partner and a young child. In contrast, Alan is mature in years, unmarried and childless and he lacks the type and range of support networks which typify other mature male students. It is these aspects of their personal and private stories that add depth to our understanding of the issues and patterns that emerge. Overall, our students suggest that maturity is a factor in choosing to teach in the first place, in their determination to complete the course and in the existence of developed support networks.

Pre-course experience and trap doors

In studies about choosing teaching as a career (Johnston *et al*, 1998, 1999; Reid and Thornton, 2000; Carrington, 2002) work experience is found to be important in generating male interest in primary teaching. Once in training our male students encounter fewer course-based problems if they have had relevant and substantial prior school experience: they then have realistic expectations of, and a strong commitment to primary teaching. For mature male students such experience, realism and commitment often comes from raising their own children but for young men the source is substantial pre-entry contact with schools. The shorter time they spend in school (a minimum of two weeks is an entry requirement), the less realistic are their expectations. Unrealistic expectations of what teaching actually involves and requires of its work force are sometimes expressed. Classically, one of Burn's (1998:9) male student's claims, 'It's not really teaching... it's easy, it's just play.'

Several of our interviewees express surprise at the workload and long hours involved.

> It is not well publicised how much work teachers do.... it is something I have realised while I have been here, just astounded by the sheer volume of work ... I think the drop-out just comes from people

coming in and going, 'my God I cannot handle this level of work'. (Will, Year 3)

Others tell how they came to choose to be teachers:

> I wanted to be a vet because, for my work experience, I went to work for a vet and that was cool ... everyone said you had to get straight A's in everything ... so I thought to myself that I would be a secretary, I don't know why ... I must have told my teachers ... because my Biology teacher ... said to me you can do much better than that, go to university. So I went and had a look through the UCAS book and there was Performing Arts, which quite appealed, and then there was Teaching and I don't know why I chose teaching really ... with Performing Arts, there wasn't a chance of me getting a job then afterwards ... so at least as a teacher I get a job. Teaching didn't leap out at me. It was a case of the other options saying 'no, boring'! (Mark, Year 4)

Both these students failed their BEd; Will had academic difficulties, failing coursework assignments, and Mark failed his teaching practice.

In HE in general, students who complete their courses tend to have been proactive in their programme choice whilst non-completers tend to have had a significant lack of commitment to their programme, or unrealistic expectations (Ozga and Sukhnandan, 1998). Similar views to Mark's can and are expressed by women students on occasions. In the public domain it is not uncommon for such views to be expressed but for those training to teach reality is quickly revealed and for some students it comes as a shock.

Coursework and teaching practice

Men students are much more likely than women to experience problems with coursework and on teaching placement. Why this may be so is debatable. Lower qualifications on entry tend to be indicative but so too might differences in approaches to studying and responses to difficulties experienced. The tendency for men to want to save face or to appear to be effortless learners may extend beyond schooling into HE. To admit failure might damage their reputation and undermine their gendered association with the successful male image.

> There is this thing of failure too. I do think men are less inclined, when they are failing, to come to someone and say I need help. I suppose it's something that's hammered into us. (Tom, BEd Year 4)

Many of our interviewees speak of other men who have left, or have failed and then retrieved parts of the course but on the whole they think that they themselves are doing OK. This general perception may not fit with that of their tutors. As Foster (1995:35) notes, there is widespread anecdotal evidence of lack of competence in male students. Nevertheless, our students tend to relate any personal difficulties to idiosyncratic events or encounters rather than to their own level of competence. One student who ultimately failed his BEd says:

> In the first year I had quite a cool supervisor who was all right, Whereas X in the second year was a complete witch! ....You couldn't relate to her at all. The third year was lovely because I was with the same teacher I was with on my deferred practice, so that was good... In the fourth year I didn't have to practice so I went into the school and I had this horrible, horrible teacher again, who I thought was going to be all right first of all. (Mo, Year 4)

Denial of difficulty emerges as a strong theme. Our respondents stress that others had difficulties, others needed help and support. There appears to be a tendency not to recognise or to hide weaknesses, to keep any problems they have to themselves (also found by Emery, 1997).

> ...Y, for example. He blew his Year 4 teaching practice... Despite the fact that X and I, for example, his little group, could see he was under stress and we were trying to reassure him, he never actually sought or requested help from us or opened up in any way ... but if the man is not going to listen he is not going to take it and there is nothing you can do. ...None of us knew about it. He never phoned any of us. (Dan, Year 4)

Teaching practice is a wake-up call for many trainees. It brings the predominance of women sharply into focus. Whilst men in training are a small minority, in primary schools it is quite possible to be the only man. Exceptions may include the headteacher, or the caretaker but the opportunity for male support and companionship is even rarer on teaching practice than it is on campus.

The relative isolation of men training to teach has been observed by others (Burn, 1998; Allan, 1993; Lewis 2002; Foster, 1995; Skelton, 1987), but our research suggests that isolation on campus may not be the only issue. Men are most likely to drop out after experiencing problems with teaching placements, suggesting that exposure to the social environment of the primary school might in itself present difficulties. The concept of centrality (Tinto, 1993) is useful in explaining this. Men on campus may have difficulty in establishing an extensive social network: there are few men on the same course and the nature of the course means that little time is available for extending social networks beyond their peers. Once on a teaching placement, social networks and personal influence are reduced even further: the student's role is not influential and when the teaching staff are almost all women, centrality is unlikely. Conversely, for women social networks are likely to be extensive, both on campus and on teaching placement.

Although none of our men say that they personally lack friends or support, most cite this as crucial to success and potentially difficult to achieve for male students due their small number and a perceived male propensity not to share their problems or difficulties with others.

> I found it good to have a friend of mine, another male, in the same school... it was fairly strange being in a female dominated profession... (It was) valuable to compare experiences, exchange ideas and enjoy the TP. (Alex BEd Year 1)

Other researchers have found that men on teaching practice are sometimes sponsored by male heads, mothered by women teachers, or nursed by their tutors (Allan, 1993; Foster, 1995; Emery, 1997; Sargent, 2001). In each case such support can help male trainees to succeed. What might be more damaging is the not infrequent barbed comments from women teachers, about teaching being an unsuitable job for men or that men see teaching only as a gateway to rapid promotion (see chapter 7). Sargent recounts many stories of this kind of pernicious banter, and Allan suggests that women teachers have a strong influence on whether male students persist in being teachers. So it is unsurprising to find that for some men teaching practice can be a make or break experience.

Patterns of experience

Whether heading for successful completion, drop-out or failure, there are some important recurring themes in men's experience of teacher training. These revolve around physical contact and suspicions of child abuse, related perceptions of being constantly scrutinised, and of simply standing out in this predominantly female domain. All these experiences can have a dramatic impact on some trainees, sometimes making them more determined to succeed, sometimes causing them to consider dropping out .

Physical contact

When men opt for primary teaching it can be perceived as un-natural, odd (Skelton, 1991). Hegemonic masculinity and homo-phobia imply that such men might be gay or paedophile and exerts considerable social pressure on men who choose to teach. Their masculinity is called into question. It seems that the younger the children, the greater the suspicion: this and other assumptions are ill-founded. Men teachers are as diverse in their masculinities as are men who do not teach. Though the majority of child abusers are men, the majority of men are not child abusers, and the most common age for children to be abused is between eight and twelve (Colton and Vanstone, 1996), which is not the age of sitting on laps, escorting to toilets and wet pants. Nevertheless, such perceptions are strongly and widely held, the corollary being that men teachers are frequently looked upon as potential child abusers.

Fear of such perceptions is common amongst our students and has been found by other researchers (Johnston *et al*, 1998, 1999; Penn and McQuail, 1997; Burn, 1998). Roy spoke of the 'fear of being accused of abuse', and Kez of being 'afraid of being called a dirty old man'.

> How a male teacher deals with a girl crying, is different to how a female teacher would deal with it and I want to see how... I need to be able to see how to deal with that in the proper recognised way... people think don't they. People always assume a lot – that scares me a little bit. (Alan, Year 2)

What trainees need are flexible and professionally oriented guidelines, focused on appropriate definitions of professional care rather than on panics about child abuse and men teachers being gay or paedophile. Unfortunately for teachers, 'guidelines for professional practice are rare and mainly relate to protection and control' (Piper and Smith, 2003:881).

School and ITE institutional input is important here. Where policies do not exist they should be devised and advice should be pro-actively given rather than waiting for it to be sought. Using Ashley and Lee's (2003) focus on *care about*, rather than *care for* in its specifically parental sense, policies about physical contact must focus on children's learning needs and be the same for men and women teachers. There is no educational or social justification for having different expectations of men and women teachers in this area of practice, whatever the moral panics might be.

Nevertheless, given the prevalence of such views and the public disgust it provokes, perceptions of men as potential child abusers are a significant deterrent for some men training to teach and on teaching practice the full force of this social opprobrium is likely to strike.

It seems naively contradictory that alongside perceptions of perversion lie public and governmental demands for more male role models, especially for boys. Students report both parental concern about young children having a male teacher and parental delight that their boys will have a male role model. Both examples carry elements of negativity. The former casts doubt on their motivations and sexuality, the later implies the stereotypical masculine behaviour of macho men. As Sargent (2000:417) cogently argues, in terms of physical contact, it is

> ... ironic that the very aspects of masculinity that ought to be modelled – responsiveness and care for children – are the very things that are most suspect.

There can be no doubt that men training to teach are vulnerable to accusations of abuse. They work in 'a climate of suspicion, characterised in part by sensational media revelations' (Williams and Jones, 2005:113). Our men, and all those training to teach, must monitor their own behaviour and ensure that none of their actions or behaviours can be misconstrued. The important point here is that rules about physical contact, whatever they are, must be based on educational reasons. We agree with Sargent (2001:29) that 'female teachers cannot be privileged over male teachers with regard to physical contact with children'. Different rules for men can push them out of teaching.

Men's perceptions of problems for men

Our students see some problems for themselves and other men – but usually other men – in teacher training. The problems they identify relate to the training context and perceived traits of men rather than the content of their training courses, with which all seem to express varying degrees of satisfaction. None seek to change course content as a means of reducing drop-out or failure rates and their suggestions for improvement focus on access to male role models and peers, not being made to stand out, and guidance on physical contact with young children.

Access to men teachers as exemplars can be addressed by placing men in male tutor groups during the campus-based part of their course, and, wherever possible, with experienced male teachers during at least some of their practice placements. The Men's Club (Appendix A4) response was to invite three successful male ex-students and two male tutors to an informal discussion at a club meeting. Access to peers was enhanced by attendance at the Club and the standing-out issue was fed back to course tutors to prompt change. In addition a new policy was adopted to ensure that men trainees were grouped together for coursework and seminars rather than being spread thinly across all tutor groups.

Physical contact is a vital issue that needs to be resolved at national level so that all teachers can be clear about what is educationally desirable and what is acceptable, regardless of teacher gender.

Male awareness of being a minority group in a female dominated profession and student cohort is strong. Their enthusiasm for the Men's Club largely focused on getting to know other male students, identifying any shared needs and getting them met.

> I've not really felt any kind of discrimination within the course, if you like, because the occasion hasn't arisen, because I've just nipped it in the bud myself. Perhaps male pride might come in to it; admission of a problem... Men tend to be more solo don't they? Women will... in general... be more gregarious as a group, a network. (Dick BEd Year 4)

These students clearly think that men are less inclined to share their feelings and experiences than women, thus confirming the male stereotype, but interestingly not one to which they belong. All but one of our respondents talked freely and openly about their lives as trainee teachers.

Standing out

Whatever the exhortations of the TDA, or public demand for more men as role models, primary teaching is not seen as masculine work and the predominance of women suggests that it is not yet masculine work: it is female work. Male students and teachers stand out: they are greeted with excitement, awe, or fear, by tutors, parents, pupils, other teachers, governors and heads because they are rare and their presence does not conform to the gender stereotypes of primary teaching.

Most of our respondents claim to be confident and experienced enough not to feel threatened by a predominantly female environment. However, as Charles (BEd Year 1) notes, the sheer number of women, in practice schools and on the training course, makes primary teaching appear to be a natural job for women which could lead to feelings of insecurity amongst male students.

The men are aware that they stand out as a small minority, but they do not want this to be exacerbated by how they are treated.

> The most important thing that you can do is not point out that there are men in the class. I think that is really bad... we had to write our name on the board to say who we were. So you wrote your name on the board and everybody said, 'Oh we know who you are. We're not going to get your name wrong because you're a man', you know, the only man in the group. So immediately I'm thinking, Oh God, I'm the only man in the group... I found it difficult in my first year... being the only male. (Tom, BEd Year 4)

Clearly it is important that tutors and teachers on placement treat all trainees as individuals rather than as representatives of a particular group, or gender. Unfortunately is not unusual for the lone man to be asked to give *the male view* on something during discussions, in contrast to the numerous and divergent views of women peers. The temptation to highlight the presence of a rare man must be resisted because it accentuates gender difference and essentialises men's views. It makes male students stand out in situations where they prefer to be treated in the same way as women peers.

Men's advice to men on getting through

These students would advise men in training to work hard and not get behind; to make friends and talk to them when they have problems and not to be afraid of asking for help, from friends or tutors. They suggest that pre-training experience is essential, to ensure that teaching is really what they want to do and to avoid mis-understandings about what teaching actually involves. Men, they say, must be encouraged to view primary teaching as a suitable career. Its image as a stereotypical, low status female occupation must be challenged and changed. Teachers in general are under-valued they say, but primary teachers especially. Men, good quality candidates especially, will not choose teaching as a career whilst it is still associated with low pay and low status.

> ... if they want to raise standards they must make teaching far more competitive, like the other professions, so you need 3 'A's to get in here please. But then you have got to have a salary, at the end of the day, to reflect that. (Dick, BEd Year 4)

> I think it's important that the status of the degree is heightened, pub-licly, because I think the more that people continue to chide and

knock at it because we're an easy target... the less respect we get and it's likely you're going to find men, who like respect, who won't want to be viewed poorly, stay away from it. (Tim, BEd Year 4)

Periphery or centre stage?

Men are in contradictory positions in teaching. As an increasingly rare commodity they are centre stage yet in this predominantly female environment they are on the periphery. Their high visibility makes them 'noticed and exposed' whilst at the same time being 'privileged and disadvantaged' (Foster, 1995:37), sidelined and glorified (Cameron, 2000). Expectations of them are both conflicting and stereotypical. Alongside such contradictions, as a small minority, it is harder for them to fit in to the predominantly female world of education programmes and school settings. Getting through teacher training can be quite difficult for them, although, as we shall see in chapter 7, once in teaching, getting on is far less problematic.

Difficulties associated with social integration have been shown to be a major influence on drop-out or course failure (Tinto, 1993). The resultant lack of centrality is as relevant for men enrolled in predominantly female Education courses as it is for the small number of women enrolled in Computer Science. The less they fit in, the looser their commitment becomes, and they are more likely to withdraw or fail. In both examples the minority groups are de-centred, on the periphery in terms of their programmes' subculture, of being able to integrate with same sex peers, and in relation to the amount of power they hold. For women doing Computer Science this is a group loss but one which likely fits with prior experiences and which accords with patriarchy and hegemonic masculinity. For men doing teaching the loss may be more keenly felt, as it runs counter to past experiences of male centrality, power and status expectations. As noted by Apple (Apple, 1990, cited Allan, 1993:126), 'The elementary school is a thoroughly gendered institution in which being male or female is an unspoken basis of power'.

For men training to teach, what is familiar is removed and replaced by something far less certain. They are much more likely to experience isolation, dislocation, personal scrutiny and a questioning of their masculinity than in any other aspect of their lives as men. It can place them under considerable pressure to display stereotypical male traits or to get out. Yet our students' reasons for wanting to teach usually run counter to such expectations.

Within teaching, at the meso and micro levels, such pressures can be addressed through activities such as the Men's Club, mentoring in schools, parental education and guidelines for behaviour. But any such action is unlikely to alter, or outweigh, the macro level expectations and pressures on men to conform to gendered expectations and stereotypes. In getting through teacher training they are likely to experience a wide range of contradictory demands. They need to be comfortable with their masculinity and well attuned to the task of teaching to survive their training.

Conclusions

Howson (cited Whittaker, 2002:20) has argued for positive discrimination for men and single-sex men-only courses 'so they don't feel intimidated', but this doesn't make long-term sense. Training requires school placement and the ability to working successfully in predominantly female environments. Segregation will not develop the necessary skills and dispositions required to work successfully with women teachers, tutors and peers.

Despite their over-representation in drop-out and failure rates, many men do get through their training successfully. It would certainly make sense for the TDA and Government to address student retention and success rates for both men and women and to treat these issues as important and worthy of extensive investment as male-focused recruitment campaigns, but single-sex courses are not the answer. Indeed, they could lead to a lowering of entrance standards, as has happened in the past (Johnstone *et al*, 1998) rather than an improvement in teacher quality and status.

What would work? We have identified some patterns that correlate with success and failure, which can be used to guide admissions and to focus support where necessary. Higher entry grades are definitely linked to successful completion of training. Young men with low entry grades are more vulnerable to problems on the course than are mature men with similar grades, and younger men tend to experience more problems when choosing to specialise in early years. Students who drift into teaching training are more likely to experience problems but this can be countered by relevant prior work experience which develops realistic expectations of what teaching actually involves, leading to higher levels of commitment. For mature men commitment may be more important than high entry qualifications.

What we have found is that men who have relevant child-related work experience, realistic expectations of what primary teaching involves and have actively chosen teaching as a career are the most committed to their course and the most likely to get through their training. Where we find lack of commitment, mirrored in some expressed reasons for entering primary ITE and instances of unrealistic expectations, men are more likely to fail. The source of the problems some men experience during training may lie within themselves.

Men training to teach are not a homogeneous group. They present a range of masculinities which are constantly negotiated and re-made during the course of their training. The impact on each student is different. Mark, described by tutors as a bit of a lad, now uses the word *lovely* to describe children's work, something he says he would never have done before. David, who appeared quiet and conscientious at Men's Club meetings, no longer feels isolated. He has seen that his commitment to primary teaching is shared by other men; he no longer feels odd. These students present quite different versions of masculinity to their pupils.

Nevertheless, public and sometimes women teachers' perceptions of men training to teach as odd, paedophile, gay or potential child abusers are serious deterrents. Such cultural and socially reinforced taboos will continue to impact on men training to teach in a disproportionate way. There is no gender advantage for men at the *getting through* stage.

Recommended reading

All the following articles address the problems male recruits to teacher education face while undergoing training.

Smedley, S. (1997) Men on the Margins: Male Student Primary Teachers, *Changing English*, 4 (2) pp217-227.

Thornton, M. (1999b), Reducing Wastage among Men Student Teachers in Primary Courses: a male club approach, *Journal of Education for Teaching*, 25:1, pp. 41-53.

Foster, T. (1995) You don't have to be Female to Succeed on this Course, but it helps, *The Redland Papers*, Bristol, University of the West of England, Autumn, 35-43.

7

Getting On

Introduction

Once qualified and in post, men in female-dominated professions achieve well, acquiring a disproportionate number of high status, senior posts. Kauppinen-Toropainen and Lammi's (1993) cross-cultural study notes this pattern in Nordic countries and the USA. Casassus (2000) reports similar disparities in France, where just 14 per cent of professors across all subjects are women, and Coleman (2002) has mapped these disparities across the United Kingdom's various educational regions and at all levels of education. It applies to health professionals as much as it does to teachers (Finlayson and Nazroo, 1998). In higher education in England, despite being 40 per cent of all academic staff, women hold just 15 per cent of vice-chancellorships and university chairs, and only 27 per cent of women in higher education are senior lecturers or researchers (Goddard, 2005:1). In secondary schools barely 31 per cent of heads are women (Powney *et al*, 2003) and in the private sector the situation is even worse: just 5 per cent of heads of co-educational secondary schools are women (Lee and Slater, 2005). Mills (2005:12) cites Australian data to show that while representing only 6 per cent of the primary teacher population, 'men constitute 22 per cent of the principal positions, 71 per cent of directors and 82 per cent of senior managers'.

Our own data from primary schools confirms this lack of proportion. Getting men into teaching is difficult, getting them through training is difficult but getting on once in teaching is not. These are clear and distinct trends within the socially structured profession of school teaching.

103

The extant literature on gender and teaching focuses on the nature of teachers work (Campbell and Neill, 1994; Nias, 1987, 1989), the *glass ceiling* effect on women seeking promotion (Wilson, 1997; Acker, 1994), the restrictions hegemonic masculinity imposes on educative and career options for men (Kenway and Willis, 1998; Mac an Ghaill, 1994; Connell, 1987) and the experience of men working in predominantly female occupations (Owen *et al*, 1998; Penn and McQuail, 1997; Ruxton, 1992). However, there is relatively little re-search into the detailed structural positioning of men within teach-ing and how they manage their careers once they are established in the profession. Alexander (1991), does include such analysis in his Leeds study, Coleman (2002) addresses it through her study of women as headteachers, and Sargent's (2001) respondents, along with many others involved in studies of men in predominantly female occupations, has described their allocation to differential roles and responsibilities, and the assignment of gendered expecta-tions to them in terms of their careers by both men and women peers. For example, men are more likely to be involved in school sports, undertake manual or technology-based tasks, take respon-sibility for high-status subjects such as Mathematics or IT (Thorn-ton, 1998) and be directed towards leadership positions or into educational administration.

In addition to a dearth of research about men's structural position-ing within teaching there are surprisingly few studies concerning the impact they might have on children's learning. A notable exception here is the recent study by the Curriculum Evaluation and Manage-ment Centre (CEM) at Durham University (Carrington *et al*, 2005). Using 1997/8 data on the performance of nine thousand ten and eleven year olds in Reading, Science and Mathematics, they found that having a man teacher had no impact on boys' attitudes to school or their achievements. What mattered was not gender but the quality of the teachers. This large scale study supports our own find-ing (see *Presence and Impact*, below), that there is little if any evi-dence to support popular assertions that more men will improve boys' achievements and behaviour in schools.

We explore patterns in men's career trajectories, appointment pro-cedures in schools, their roles and responsibilities, and their impact as men on school effectiveness. By looking at men who are getting on in teaching, locating the spaces they occupy and exploring the impact they have on pupil achievement it is possible to assess whether or not education does need more of them: the other side of the missing men conundrum. They may be missing but are they missed?

Teaching as a gendered occupation

Bradley (1993) outlines the history and centrality in feminist scholarship of occupational sex-typing and its importance in our 'understanding of gender relations and of power disparities between men and women'. While recognising significant variation in gendered occupations across time and place, what remains common is that its incidence is 'widespread and pervasive' (Bradley, 1993:11). Citing Hakim's (1979) renowned statistical study, she points to the pervasiveness of 'horizontal segregation' in terms of occupations, where men and women choose different fields of work such as engineering or nursing, and 'vertical segregation' in terms of senior positions, where men manage women, and their endurance over time. The issue of teaching as a gendered occupation and its endurance over time is amply illustrated in chapter 3 of this book.

Using the USA and the UK as examples Bradley (1993) identifies three generic styles of male entry into predominantly female occupations:

i)   *Takeover*, where men replace women as the main employees

ii) *Invasion*, where increased numbers of men results in internal demarcation, the occupation of different spaces (e.g. subject specialisms, age phases, roles and responsibilities) and higher status/more powerful positions (disproportionate headships in schools and leadership roles in higher education and beyond);

iii) *Infiltration*, where few men enter for personal reasons, such as few occupational alternatives or a distaste for stereotypical masculine environments.

As with *invasion*, men entering female occupations through *infiltration* may exploit, or be encouraged to exploit, opportunities to advance their careers. Some men entering teaching reject this view, expressing a desire to teach and remain at the chalk face (Johnston *et al*, 1998; Sargeant, 2001; Thornton and Bricheno, 2000) Others enter because they do envisage rapid promotion to senior positions (Thornton and Bricheno, 2000), whilst others still are propelled, reluctant or otherwise, into leadership positions by the actions and sponsorship of significant others such as headteachers, governors, appointment panels, mentors and peers by virtue of their maleness. Similar patterns can be seen in occupations such as nursing, where women also predominate (Floge and Merrill, 1986). Our data suggest that men entering teaching have indeed invaded the profession, in the sense of disproportionately taking on different and higher status positions to women despite a decline in their numbers. This invasion occurs alongside infiltration, where some men, as we saw in chapter 6, just want to teach regardless of the social opprobrium that may attach to them.

Career trajectories

One of our early small-scale surveys of twenty two primary schools (Thornton, 1996; Appendix A1), identified a large proportion of men reaching headship or deputy head level. We found that they often had high status subject responsibilities such as Mathematics, Science and ICT and that they usually taught the oldest children (ten to eleven year olds). A follow up survey of 390 primary schools in Hertfordshire (Thornton, 1999a; Appendix A2) and our later large-scale National Survey's (Thornton and Bricheno, 2000; Appendix A5) confirm these findings. As we can see in Table 1 below, in a sample of 1872, of whom 250 are men, the majority of women (61%) are on main professional grade (MPG), holding no additional allowances or management positions and that the majority of men (65%) are on salaries above MPG, as allowance holders or as part of the senior management team. Over a third of the men have achieved headship, whilst only 7 per cent of women have done so. There may be relatively few men in this sample (13%: 250) but once qualified and in post they certainly appear to have excellent prospects in terms of getting on.

In this study significant differences (p<0.001) are found between men and women teachers and school type (infant, first, junior, middle and primary schools). Men are mostly teaching in, and head-

Table 1 Gender distribution and teaching position (Thornton, 1999a)

	Male (250)	Female (1622)
Heads	35%	7%
Deputies	17%	9%
Allowance Holders	13%	23%
Not-Allowance Holders	32%	53%
Floating (no class)	3%	8%
Total	100%	100%

teachers of, schools that contain older children, whilst women teachers are spread much more evenly across age-phases. Well over 80 per cent of men in these Hertfordshire schools either teach eight to eleven year olds (KS2) or are headteachers. More than two-thirds of men KS2 teachers teach the oldest children (aged ten and eleven), whilst less than 17 per cent of men work with three to seven year olds.

In Loizou and Rossiter's (1987) study, their finding, that 'most maths post-holders were teaching in the upper years of primary school', was not subject to further explanation. However, Alexander (1991) examined in some detail the status and gender of post-holders for the seven most frequently co-ordinated curriculum areas in a representative sample of thirty Leeds schools. He found that 'all male maths post-holders were of a higher status than MPG', and they received additional salary in the form of an incentive allowance. Women teachers on MPG held posts of responsibility for Maths in half of schools, which meant they received no extra salary for doing so, but '...in only 3 of the 17 schools which had any male staff *at all* were women rather than men responsible for maths' (p131, our emphasis). This is significant: it suggests that if men are available then they, rather than women, will be assigned responsibility for Maths. In addition, Alexander found that 'A third of the sample's deputies co-ordinated maths', and 38 per cent of the sample's deputies were men. He states

> ....schools in the sample consistently gave priority to developing curriculum areas co-ordinated by high status teachers (e.g. deputy heads and allowance holders), and these areas tended to have a high proportion of male teachers holding responsibility.... (p135)

Alexander's findings parallel our own. In each case there is a strong connection between subject specialism, age-range taught, power position and being a male teacher. In addition, his work suggests that if women are in competition with men for these posts, they are less likely to get them and if they do get them then they are less likely to get a salary increase. This is not based on qualifications held: we have qualification data for our sample (Thornton and Bricheno, 2000) but can find no evidence to suggest that men and women teachers are differentially qualified for the positions they hold.

For primary teachers in England and Wales, as elsewhere, higher status (and subsequent authority, power and salary) goes with the teaching of older pupils and being men. As Skelton (1991) notes, the younger the child the lower the status of its teacher. This power/

status pattern is illustrated by the gender distribution of teachers not only between schools (different age-phases) but also within schools, by age and by subject. Whilst primary teaching may be the extreme example of gender differences in teaching, similar patterns emerge when studies in secondary schools are undertaken. 69 per cent of secondary heads are men even though 55 per cent of secondary teachers are women (Powney *et al*, 2003). The gendered patterns of 'getting on' in a teaching career are repeated at all levels of education.

Career perceptions

Our qualitative data from the National Careers Survey (Thornton and Bricheno, 2000; Appendix A5) also suggest some important gender disparities in primary teachers' perceptions of their careers, priorities, orientation to work and the opportunities that they believe are available to them. For some men progression to headship is seen as the logical way for their careers to develop.

> That it was always a natural progression and what I set out to do. It seems that if you enter a profession you should seek to 'aim for the top'. (Male, 269.1)

> Look forward to more challenge. Able to lead/decision making. (Male, 88.2)

For other men there is a shared concern with some women peers about headship taking them away from the prime purpose of the job i.e. teaching and the children.

> Headship (and deputy headships in large schools) is more and more becoming a managerial/financial type of job, to the exclusion of contact with children. I would not seek promotion unless I could guarantee a large proportion of my time involved some input into day-to-day teaching. I also think that the position of head carries far too much power – the role of an SMT (Senior Management Team) should be developed and some of the head's powers devolved to it (Male, 194.7)

> Promotion is often seen as a reward for work done on cultivating contacts, doing courses, which may or may not be relevant to real classroom needs, and other 'band-wagon' stuff. Next for me is some voluntary work: i.e. my own children are GCSE + University. Soon I'll be free to teach someone who will thank me, somewhere in the world outside UK Promotion for me is not an option. (Male, 269.3)

Clearly, not all men as individuals seek the power and status of headship or enact traits of hegemonic masculinity (Connell, 1987).

Women tend to argue that to take on more senior roles they have to be able to delegate to a partner or extended family and that this is a stronger possibility for men with female partners at home than it is for women. They also recognise that regaining career momentum once they have had a career break to have and raise children is difficult for them. No doubt this is a factor in women heads being far more likely to be single than their male peers. Almost all male head-teachers (98%) have domestic partners whilst one in three female heads lives alone (Thornton, 2001; Powney *et al*, 2003). Not surprisingly women emphasise men's career advantages.

> The workload is making promotion accessible to those who do not have family commitments. This limits it to mainly men and excludes working mums for the most part. (Female 92.2)

> ...it could be easier for a man, men can almost drift into things and are often not restricted by their families. (Gavin, Male Headteacher)

Such apparent and often cited individual female resentment of the gendered nature of career opportunities is largely unrecognised by most men we surveyed, although our interview data suggest that when men are engaged in open discussion, some men recognise the possibility of a gendered career advantage. Without that dialogue men do not acknowledge that gender is an advantage in their careers. Women clearly do!

There are clear patterns of men disproportionately getting on in teaching: their career trajectories generally indicate appointment to higher status and higher paid positions, virtually no career breaks and traditionally fewer family responsibilities. Apart from partner support in the home, what helps them move forward so regularly? Why do men ascend the glass escalator whilst women hit the glass ceiling? (Benton DeCorse and Vogtle, 1997; Williams, 2000). An understanding of appointment and promotions procedures might help to explain this.

Appointments, promotions, and the role of governors
Appointments and promotions

Even as newly qualified teachers (NQTs) men seem to have an advantage. Our male students are aware of their rarity value and some plan to use this to further their careers.

> Its one of those things. Because there's a shortage of males... schools are more likely to push you ahead... in order to keep those males. But if you boost the amount of men in the profession then career prospects drop. (Tom, BEd Year 4)

> I've also got another school chasing me already so I'm going to play two ends against each other and I'm going to see if I can't get some financial benefit. (Dick, BEd Year 4)

Daniel managed to progress his career through personal contact and some special treatment. He heard about an early years vacancy at a school where he had previous experience and mentioned it to the school secretary whom he knew outside the school situation.

> I said, 'Oh, you've got a vacancy coming up' and I said, 'I would be in it like a shot but you couldn't afford me'. But the head rang me the next day and said it's your job if you want it... I came into the interview and I could see all the governors were under strict instructions not to ask me any difficult questions. It was nice although not a particularly democratic way of doing it of course... I was well qualified for the job and they needed someone to sort the IT out and I have got a large, huge amount of IT experience, and they needed someone in early years who was interested in it and that was me.

Simply being men and being rare seems to help in the early stages of their careers. So too might career intentions. In all our studies men generally report a different pattern of career intentions from women who have similar qualifications and length of service. Many men, though not all, want and seek promotion (Thornton and Bricheno, 2000). The data suggest a firmness of decision-making for men that is not necessarily shared by women. Men appear more likely to apply for promotion and to get it! However, we do not adhere to the myth that women teachers lack commitment or desire for promotion (Measor and Sikes, 1992; Coleman, 2002). There is some evidence that women are more cautious in their applications, wanting to be sure that they have the right experience and qualifications before applying and that men are more likely to be overly confident and proactive. Cubillo, (1999) in her study of applicants to the National Programme for Qualified Head Teachers, found that men are hyper-confident in self-rating their abilities but women are more cautious. There is also evidence that men, more than women, are actively encouraged to seek promotion (Coleman, 2002; Sargent, 2001). And women considering promotion are more likely to cite constraints such as the combination of family responsibilities and work loads, which are already too high for many of them. There is also considerable evidence in our data that many women who apply for promotion experience bias against them.

> I do feel in early years that men have an unfair advantage as I remember attending an interview for a post 'experienced infant teacher required'. All the candidates were female apart from the one male who was straight out of uni (versity) and needless to say he was appointed! (Female, 68.5)

Coleman's recent study (2002) of almost a thousand secondary school headteachers suggests that almost 63 per cent of women have experienced gender bias in teaching appointments and that their efforts to seek promotion are often blocked by male dominated interview panels and sexist governors.

> ... they started off the interview by saying we apologise for the fact that we're all men here, but that's just a challenge for you. I remember thinking, 'yes, well if I go and get the job, it's going to be a challenge for you as well'. (p39)

Her respondents cite reasons given them for not being promoted, such as wearing too much jewellery or being too short, and her study confirms earlier research (Southworth, 1990, Thornton and Bricheno, 2000) that women applicants are often treated differently to men, perhaps being asked about their plans for marriage or having children and their partners' views about them working. One of our headteacher respondents, Nancy, said 'Oh it's good for men to be forceful and dominant but it's not good for women to be. And you don't go to interviews in trousers!'

Governing bodies

Teacher interview panels consist of disproportionate numbers of men, either as senior or headteachers or as governors and local authority representatives (Coleman, 2002:42). In schools in England and Wales, governing bodies have a great deal of power, making and influencing decisions about promotion, appointments and pay. They involve, alongside headteachers and civil servants or politicians, volunteer lay people from the community and local businesses and parents. Training for school governorship is encouraged but is optional, and equality or gender issues are not high on the agenda of governor training (Bagley, 1993; Thornton, 2000b). Thus traditional attitudes, such as having men in leadership roles, can go unchallenged and the small number of available men teachers can lead school governors to favour men when considering appointments and promotions in their schools.

... all things being equal they would choose the men, because the governors would want to choose a man because they wanted a man in their school. (Geoff, Headteacher)

Our women teachers (Appendix A5) are quite strong in their criticism of governors on appointment and promotion panels.

I felt the interview had gone well and the governors took a long time in deliberating, and when they came back in and took the chappie away I said 'can I have feedback please', and the diocesan man and the education office man fed back, and I said 'right, what have I got to do to improve' and they said 'nothing', and they said, 'I want you to think about the quirky nature of governing bodies', in other words, yes, they wanted a male teacher. (Alison, Headteacher)

Several cited governor's lack of training for the role:

I think that they need training in their responsibilities and in how to do things, and they need advice... there's a lot of governor training on offer and part of the budget was two hundred and fifty pounds in the budget for governor training, it would cost them nothing... I cannot get them ever to do any of these courses... (Nancy, Head-teacher)

When women succeed in becoming headteachers, the traditional attitudes and behaviour of some governors continues to impact on them, and on appointments and promotions within their schools. Several women heads report the constant need to monitor governors who wish to include extraneous gender criteria in their appointment decisions.

I was on an interview panel and a governor, against express instructions said something to a woman about being a single parent, how could she cope if her child was ill, and three or four of us all at the same time said, 'Excuse me, you don't answer that question, it's not on'. (Nancy, Headteacher)

... the first interview I ever did I stopped it and asked if he (the Chair of Governors) minded stepping outside the room. He asked this woman first of all about child care and I was too flabbergasted to stop him, and then he said, 'How are you going to arrange it so you don't get caught in the traffic?' (Becky, Headteacher)

Current proposals for a new Equality Bill in autumn 2005, that requires organisations to address inequalities in employment and pay, amazingly seek to exempt schools and teachers, because of government fears that it will inhibit single-sex teaching strategies which might enhance the performance of boys (Slater, 2005). This is a retrograde step since past equal opportunities legislation has to a large extent limited the opportunity for overt discrimination in favour of men. Nevertheless, there is much evidence that covert discrimination still occurs, with men prioritised for advancement as breadwinners, role models, to handle discipline and boys' games, sort out the technology, or as academically rather than pastorally gifted (Evetts, 1989, Coleman, 2002). The new legislation, if passed, is likely to aggravate this.

It is not inevitable, and it may not always be the case but current evidence suggests that in general, within education:

- men take priority in promotion appointments
- promotion procedures actually work in favour of men (no career breaks, traditional views of some governors who are disproportionately men)
- men seek, or come under pressure to seek senior management roles which usually remove them from the classroom and contact with children
- men are less likely to be lone parents or to have such extensive family commitments as their women peers
- men are still seen as the chief bread-winners

Men in teaching work in an increasingly female profession, but within it they continue to acquire disproportionately high status leadership positions. Gendered inequalities in power in education flow from this educational division of labour. In this context it is wise to remember Bernstein's (1972) dictum: schools cannot compensate for society. Equal opportunities policies and legislation originating in the 1970s appear to have had little impact on patterns of teacher stratification by gender in our schools and new legislation may reinforce this.

Subject specialism

Primary teachers are predominantly perceived and labelled as generalists, secondary teachers as specialists. However, secondary teachers may be more accurately described as subject specialists and primary teachers as primary specialists. In common language use, despite their distinctive areas of professional knowledge and skills, primary teachers are either explicitly described as non-specialists or implicitly deemed such through the use of the term specialist to describe only subject specialist teachers (secondary and higher education). When successive Secretaries of State for Education call for more specialist teaching in primary schools, they are calling for more subject teaching. The selective use of the term specialist directly indicates differential status, with primary teachers' traditional areas of expertise effectively devalued in relation to their secondary colleagues. Men are more inclined to seek high status positions (see chapter 14), and are more subject-oriented than women training to teach so the classification of primary teaching as non-specialist in subject terms can be an additional deterrent for men.

A key feature in the educational division of labour is the differential power base of the two teacher specialisms. Both grew and developed relatively independently of the other (Thornton, 1998):

- subject specialism was originally located in the public and grammar school traditions
- primary specialism grew out of and was adapted from the elementary school tradition

The prioritisation of subject over primary specialism is not the result of an evolutionary process (Durkheim, 1965) but rather of an educational and ideological struggle based upon different socially located educational philosophies and epistemologies, supported by different social and political groups. The outcome of this struggle has been the prioritisation of subject specialism. Following the introduction of the National Curriculum (1998), the educational division of labour based on it, although not new to primary education, has become more firmly entrenched.

Within primary education, as in education in general, there is a well established hierarchy of subject disciplines with Science, Mathematics and ICT ranked above Human Sciences and the Arts. Alexander's research in Leeds (1991) confirms the presence of this hierarchy in the primary curriculum and its direct relationship to the hierarchical division of labour between primary teachers. Subject specialisms across all age ranges correlate strongly with teacher gender and positions of seniority (Thornton, 1998; Thornton and Bricheno, 2000; Alexander, 1991).

The relationship between gender and subjects studied by pupils is also well documented. Despite some narrowing of gaps in recent years and clear improvements for girls across many curriculum areas, boys remain more likely than girls to study Maths, Technology and Science based subjects to advanced levels , and girls are more likely to do the same in Humanities and Arts based subjects. This difference is replicated in the gender distribution of secondary school and higher education subject-based teachers. The situation in primary schools now mirrors this, despite its principle of teachers covering the whole curriculum through class teaching and despite the predominance of women teachers. As we have shown, men are disproportionately more likely to take responsibility for high status subjects, even if these are not their areas of expertise, and to receive extra pay for doing so. Women are disproportionately more likely to take responsibility for non-subject based areas of responsibility, such as SEN, assessment or a particular age-phase, such as KS1 (Thornton and Bricheno, 2000).

Further research into the staff gender balance in primary schools (Bricheno and Thornton, 2002; Appendix A7) has suggested that men teachers are not only more likely to take responsibility for high status subjects and the teaching of older children but are also more likely to be found in large schools with male heads than in small schools with female heads. Despite this positioning we can find no discernable relationship between staff gender and pupil achievement in the high status subjects that are subject to annual testing in primary schools. Issues of male presence and impact need to be examined to gauge the effect men 'getting on' has on their schools and the achievements of their pupils.

Getting on: presence and impact

There are always exceptions to the patterns we find. While men as teachers are increasingly rare, sometimes they can be found in abundance, a bit like all the buses coming along at once. One such exception is a primary school in Oxford which, in 2002, had seven men teachers working under a woman headteacher (Wilce, 2002). The head argues that men are more likely to apply to schools where there are already men, so that there is something of a snowball effect, and that more men would consider primary teaching if they knew what is was really like on the ground. She advertises on the internet because that is where men are likely to look for jobs, and emphasises aspects of teaching that may attract men, such as 'toys for boys', like the increasing use of interactive white boards in schools. Her purpose in seeking to employ more men is so that children experience men and women working together and learn from them that men as well as women can be kind, caring and fair. In this way she presents men teachers as positive role models for children.

Men teachers can also be seen in less than positive ways, certainly as role models for boys, but also as examples of patriarchy and hegemonic masculinity, where men are competitive, sport-oriented, aggressive and dominate women (Flintoff, 1993). Teachers do model adult roles to their pupils and in doing so present different versions of masculinity and femininity. This can convey particular messages to pupils, namely that men do have greater power and status than women and that men lead and manage women. Emphasising men's career advantages, which are widely modelled in English schools today, could be a useful, if morally questionable, strategy for getting more men into teaching.

Male presence

Within our sample of 846 schools nation-wide (Bricheno and Thornton, 2002; Appendix A7), 30 per cent had no male teachers at all and less than 42 per cent had a male headteacher (Table 1).

Table 1: Number of schools with no male teachers and gender of head teacher.

	Headteacher		Schools with no male teachers	
	n	%	n	%
Male head teacher	349	41.3	86	10.2
Female head teacher	497	58.7	171	20.2
Total	846	100	257	30.4

We found that gender balance is related to the type of school and to the gender of the headteacher (Figure 1); where there is a male head there are more likely to be male teachers. The snowball effect of men working in schools where there are other men is thus supported by our data. Only 10 per cent of male-headed schools had no other male teachers while in female-headed schools 20 per cent had no male teachers.

Men headteachers are more likely to be found in primary and junior schools than in first, infant or lower schools. Our findings confirm research undertaken by Edwards and Lyons (1994, 1996). They too found that men are much more likely to be headteachers in both primary and secondary schools. In the primary sector they are more likely to lead junior schools with older children, and the biggest schools which give them more pay and promotion opportunities. This pattern gets stronger the further one moves away from the capital city. Their research found that 'the further one moves from London the greater the tendency for the age of pupils and the size of school to be directly related to the gender of the head' (1996, p2).

In terms of gender equity it appears that urban and city areas are much more likely to have proportionate representation of men and women headteachers, unlike in regional areas (Coleman, 2002).

The tendency for men to gravitate towards other men is most dramatically illustrated by the rare cases when men head up first, infant or lower schools. In such instances we found that 12 per cent of staff are male compared to around just 5 per cent in similar female-headed schools.

Figure 1: The gender balance by school type and gender of head

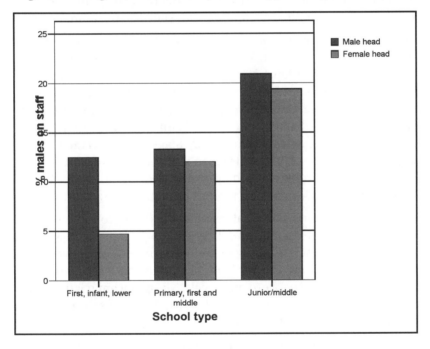

Given the tendency for men to be more career-focused than women, it is not surprising that they appear to gravitate towards larger schools which inevitably have more promotion opportunities and bigger budgets. As one of our women respondents commented:

> Often working in a small school can limit opportunities of promotion as there is insufficient structure within a school for movement and progression. Also lack of money for promotion opportunities does not encourage incentives. You are expected to take on

a wide range of tasks for no more pay or opportunity. Larger schools usually provide more opportunities and scope for development within their structure. (65.3)

Male impact

We have found that the achievements of pupils in primary schools appear to be unaffected by the proportion of men in a school, as have Carrington *et al* (2005). Similarly, Martin and Marsh (2005) have found no evidence that for junior and middle high school pupils in Australia, boys do better in terms of academic motivation and engagement, with male rather than female teachers. Our data suggest that in larger schools pupil achievement tends to be lower (Appendix A7), but simple correlation coefficients do not take account of other factors, such as the school type, the number of free meals or the percentage of children with special educational needs.

Regression analysis, taking account of school size, number of free meals, and the percentage of children with special educational needs found no relationship between the gender balance of teaching staff and Key Stage 2 test results. However, there was a relationship between KS 2 results and the percentage of children having special educational needs and a significant relationship was found for *all* curriculum areas and both Key Stage results relating to the percentage of free school meals taken in the school, suggesting that a child's background is likely to be more important than the gender of their teacher in its effect on their examination performance.

Only two significant statistical relationships were found. One between the size of the school and the gender balance – the bigger the school the more men teaching in them. The other was between the size of the school and the performance indicators – the bigger the school the lower the performance levels. No significant relationships are found between teacher gender balance and KS2 test results (all 846 schools) or KS1 test results (in 106 schools).

It would be wrong to assume that big schools produce a lower performance level because they often have more men teachers. Lower performance in larger schools is more likely to be related to socio-economic factors than to teacher gender; larger schools are generally to be found in inner-city areas where free school meals numbers and the incidence of special educational needs (SEN) tend to be higher (the greater the proportion of free school meals taken and SEN, the lower the KS results), (Carrington *et al*, 2005; Bricheno and Thornton, 2002).

However, we did find that KS2 performance indicators were significantly related to standards of behaviour, as judged by Ofsted inspections: the better the behaviour the higher the test results.

Figure 2: The relationship between gender balance and Ofsted behaviour grades

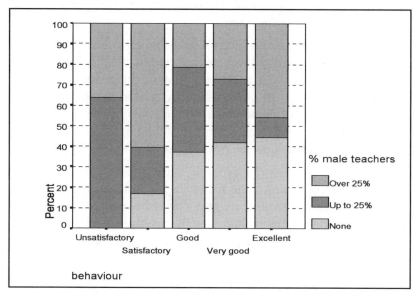

In a sample of 112 schools matched to their Ofsted reports we found:

- a significant correlation between Ofsted judgements of pupil behaviour and staff gender balance (Spearman's, $p = 0.032$), suggesting that behaviour may be less good in schools where there are more men

- no reports of unsatisfactory behaviour in female only schools

- behaviour was judged to be excellent in a large proportion of schools which were female only

- that the social background of the school seems to be more important than the gender balance of teaching staff in its effect on behaviour or on achievement

The significant relationship between gender balance and behaviour is of particular interest since one of the arguments for more men is that boys' behaviour would improve if there were more of them. Our data suggest the opposite: that behaviour seems to be better in solely or predominantly female schools and not as good in schools with higher proportions of men. However, it may well be school size rather than the teacher gender balance that causes this. Behaviour may be better in small schools *per se,* rather than the large ones to which men seem to gravitate. We must be tentative about this because of the limited research in this area and also because data is dependent upon Ofsted judgements, which are regarded as subjective and unreliable. Individual case studies are likely to provide more valuable insights into this issue.

Factors such as the size of school and the socio-economic background of the pupils might well be expected to affect behaviour. For the 95 schools included in this latter analysis the gender balance of the staff appears not to be significantly related to behaviour ($p= 0.067$). But the level of significance is not far beyond the 0.05 level, so it is possible that gender balance may still be implicated in Ofsted judgements of behaviour, even when social disadvantage is taken into account.

Ofsted judgements about the leadership abilities of headteachers also differ significantly and suggest that women may make better leaders of primary schools than men. In a sample of 419 schools:

- women are more likely to be judged to have better leadership skills (Chi squared tests: $p = 0.015$)

- newly appointed heads are more likely to be judged to have better leadership skills (Chi squared tests: $p= 0.004$)

- 62 per cent of new headteachers are women

The use of Key Stage test results to make comparisons between schools has been widely criticised for failing to take account of pupils' prior achievements, their socio-economic background and mobility. And Ofsted judgements have been criticised for their lack of reliability and validity (Fidler *et al,* 1998; Goldstein, reported by Pyke, 1998; Fitz-Gibbon and Stephenson-Forster, 1999), mainly because they draw largely on qualitative data and there are always alternative interpretations of the same school (Gray and Wilcox, 1995). On the other hand, league tables and Ofsted reports are the only sources of comparable data from every state primary school in England and as such are worthy of examination and comparison with the proviso that background variables must be taken into account and Ofsted judgements must be viewed as informed but subjective opinions.

Summary of male presence and impact

Given all these provisos we would argue that:

- staff gender balance is related to school size and school type, with more men to be found in larger schools, junior schools and those headed by men

- there is no discernable direct relationship between staff gender balance and overall school performance indicators at KS 2

- the social background of the school seems to be more important than staff gender balance, in its effect on behaviour or achievement

- pupil behaviour in a school *may* be related to staff gender balance as schools with more women are judged to have better standards of behaviour

- school leadership appears to be significantly better if the headteacher is a woman

Without doubt, these findings raise questions about government assertions that more male teachers are needed to boost the academic performance and behaviour of boys.

It might seem obvious that teacher gender balance may have important implications for the effects that schools have on their pupils' educational outcomes. However, given the weight and extent of educational and school-based research into boys' and girls' achievements, government policy to raise standards and TDA strategies to recruit more men (TTA, 2003 and 2004), it is remarkable how rarely teacher gender has been addressed as a variable within school-based educational research and school improvement initiatives. We can find no evidence that supports the assertion that more men teachers would help improve boys' achievements. If the assertion is correct one might reasonably expect to detect generally lower standards of achievement in schools with few men and higher standards when there are more men. This has not been borne out in our research. Other variables clearly intervene and there is some tentative indication that in primary education at least, more women may result in better behaviour and school leadership.

Conclusions: do we miss men?

The educational division of labour that permeates teaching cannot be understood in isolation from the complex and changing social, political and economic contexts in which it is located. Teachers, as workers, are socially located. They do not exist in a social vacuum, in an idealised world, in an education system divorced from its social location. That men get on in teaching parallels male dominance in wider society. They acquire disproportionate power and status. Gender and status issues inevitably permeate their work and social world, whether they want them to or not. Men as teachers are constrained by formal political demands, and informal and formal social expectations. The roles, responsibilities and career paths they adopt are an outcome of socially structured possibilities that partly reflect and result from gendered relationships of domination and subordination in society, from the differential distribution of power resources. It is not surprising, therefore, that the gendered stratification of teachers occurs along age-range taught, school size, subject and status lines and is reflected in men's and women's career trajectories. The appointments and promotions process is but one example. It may appear to be school-located but such processes are permeated by wider social influences, not least those that impinge upon lay governors and politicians.

We have explored men's presence in schools, their career trajectories, appointment procedures and the impact they may have on school leadership, achievement and pupil behaviour. There can be little doubt that when in teaching men are successful in getting on. Theirs is a glass escalator in terms of career intentions and the expectations and support of others. They are most definitely not missing from management and leadership roles in education. Indeed, Ofsted reports suggest that it may well be a case of missing women when it comes to leadership and behaviour management in our schools.

Whether schools and the pupils in them are missing something important by having relatively few men teachers is a quite different question. The impact of teacher gender on pupil achievement is an under-researched area but evidence suggests that it has no discernible effect. Good teaching is much more important than the gender of the teacher or headteacher.

Are men missed for other reasons? Perhaps. No doubt it is important for future generations to see teaching as a good job for both men and women, for there to be a better gender balance in teaching as a whole and in subject affiliation, age-range taught and leadership positions. It is also important that children experience men and women performing counter-stereotypical roles and the infinite variety of masculinities and femininities that lie between the two extremes. Men disproportionately occupying managerial roles or exhibiting traits of hegemonic masculinity will not be missed in teaching but their more enlightened brothers will be.

Recommended reading

Marianne Coleman's, *Women as Headteachers: Striking the balance* (Trentham Books, 2002) provides a thorough and detailed overview of the imbalance between men and women's career trajectories in education, based on over 1,000 responses from secondary headteachers.

Sandra Acker's, classic *Gendered Education* (OU Press, 1994), particularly Part 2; Women and Teaching, offers powerful insights into male advantage in educational careers.

The impact of men on school outcomes is directly addressed in Bricheno P., and Thornton, M., (2002) Staff gender balance in primary schools, *Research in Education*, No. 68, p57-64.

8
Getting Out

Introduction

Concerns have been expressed by government, House of Commons Education and Skills Committee, 2004, about recruitment and retention in the teaching workforce: a survey of teacher resignations and recruitment from 1985/6 to 2003 (Employers Organisation for Local Government, 2004) found that the percentage of full-time permanent teachers leaving the profession in both primary and secondary schools has increased. Smithers and Robinson, (2001:38) note that 18 per cent of teachers leave after just three years of teaching. More recently Halpin (2005:29) said:

> As many as 40 per cent of teachers were leaving some secondary schools every year, while one London primary suffered a 200 per cent turnover of staff. Movement away from schools in London was twice the national average.

The small proportion of men entering the profession has been explored in chapter 3. In this chapter we look at those leaving teaching. For many men, once they have entered the teaching profession, there are good opportunities for career progression; promotions and a good salary are more likely to be achieved by men than by women, as shown in chapter 7. But what about those who decide that teaching is not for them? Are men more likely to leave the profession than women? What motivates men – and women – to leave teaching and what do they do instead? We have demonstrated that there are differences between men and women in recruitment to teaching, successfully completing training and in the subsequent progress of their careers. But what about those leaving the profession, are there gender differences here too?

Our interest here is in those leaving the profession, rather than simply moving to another school. The DfES and the Employers' Organisation use the terms turnover and wastage in connection with teacher resignations; turnover is resignations from individual schools, some of which can be to move on to other schools, but wastage is loss from the maintained sector. So wastage refers to leavers.

One third of teachers have expressed a desire to leave the profession over the next five years (MORI, 2002). Smithers and Robinson (2004) find that women are more likely to resign and also to leave teaching than men. In 2004 only 16 per cent of primary teachers were male and an even smaller percentage of men held part-time or fixed term contacts: only 4 per cent of part-time staff in primary schools are male. Part-time and fixed term posts are usually those most at risk of disappearing; in addition many women leave teaching, even if they intend to return later, to take maternity leave, so it is unsurprising that more women than men feature in resignation figures. Smithers and Robinson (2005) note that early retirement accounts for over a third of headteacher resignations in both primary and secondary schools and that resignations among women teachers in primary schools are dominated by maternity leave or moving to another school.

However, in terms of wastage rates, Figure 1 shows clearly that it is higher at primary than at secondary level and for women than for men. Although the trend for wastage appears to be similar for men and women in secondary schools, it has risen steeply and consistently for men in primary schools since 1999.

These figures raise interesting questions about who leaves teaching and why they leave. Why is there such a steep increase in the leaving rates among male primary school teachers, and do men and women leave teaching for different reasons?

Departures

A review of research undertaken for the TTA in 2000 (Spear *et al*, 2000) suggests that those leaving the profession do so as a result of high workload, poor pay and low status and morale. Primary teachers are less satisfied than their secondary colleagues with their work-life balance but secondary teachers feel that they have less influence on school policy. Barmby and Coe's review (2004) concludes that the important factors affecting retention include: workload, government initiatives, stress, pupil behaviour, pay and school

Figure 1: Male and female wastage 1999-2004

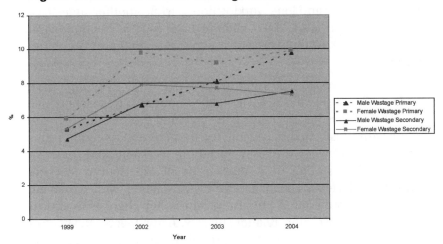

(Source: Smithers and Robinson, 2005; 2001)

management. Workload and pay feature in both these reviews but it is interesting to note the presence of new factors in the later review. Although stress has been a recurring issue in teacher retention (Smithers and Robinson, 2004; Sturman, 2002), school management and pupil behaviour are relatively new concerns. Do these differences indicate that the pressures of teaching have changed in recent years?

A number of large-scale surveys have been conducted since the review by Spear *et al* (2000), as well as a few smaller-scale qualitative studies. Hutchings *et al* (2002) survey of 1278 teachers, leaving or joining London schools, found that a third of those leaving cited pupil behaviour as a reason for leaving, whether they were taking up another post or leaving the profession. Issues relating to school management and poor leadership were the most frequently cited reasons for leaving. The National Foundation for Educational Research found that while teachers' job satisfaction was higher than those in comparable professions, teachers were concerned about work-related stress. (Sturman, 2002). In 2002 MORI surveyed over 70,000 registered members of the GTC and found that the most demotivating factors for those currently teaching were: workload, initiative overload and the target-driven culture. Smithers and Robinson's (2003) survey of 1578 teachers who were leaving found that workload and stress were particularly important and pay the least important. Powney *et al*'s (2003) study of over 2000 teachers across sixteen LEAs, found that the most common reasons given for thinking of leaving were heavy workload, too much paperwork stress of teaching and long working hours, while another large-scale survey (Sturman *et al*, 2005) identified the biggest frustrations in teaching as lack of time, excessive paperwork, and poor pupil behaviour.

Three qualitative studies using interviews and focus groups have made similar observations. MORI (2001) found that ex-teachers give a number of reasons for quitting the teaching profession which are in line with those cited as causing recruitment and retention problems by interviewees generally, including workload and initiative overload. Case studies of a small group of experienced teachers (Wilkins and Head, 2002) identify dissatisfaction with workload, status and remuneration but also recent policy changes in education and poor working relationships with managers. Bush *et al* (2005), working with eleven focus groups of teachers in *Challenging Schools* (seven in London), find that the most crucial issues are leadership and management, poor behaviour, and pay.

Workload, including long working hours and excessive paperwork and pay, are common to all of these studies. Stress, school management and pupil behaviour are important factors in most of them and there are new reasons which arise directly from government initiatives: the target-driven culture, inspections, policy initiatives and the effects of increased centralised control of the curriculum.

Leavers' reasons

Besides our own recent work, (Appendix A10) only two studies appear to have sought the views of teachers who are about to leave or have already left (Hutchings *et al*, 2002; Smithers and Robinson, 2003). Our study specifically asks those who are leaving or have already left the profession to tell us their reasons for leaving. We find many reasons in common with other surveys but also some quite striking differences. These differences may be accounted for by the nature of the sample and its methodology: a self selecting sample of teachers who felt strongly enough to respond to national advertisements which invited completion of an on-line survey and which are deliberately targeted at teachers who have left or are thinking of leaving. This survey of 371 teachers and ex-teachers also finds that pupil behaviour is most often mentioned (40%). However, workload is mentioned less frequently than government initiatives (25% as opposed to 35%) as a reason for leaving. Poor management, paperwork and stress are the reasons reported for leaving more often than pay.

Table 2: Top ten reasons given for leaving the teaching profession

Reason for leaving	Number of teachers	% of teachers
Pupil behaviour	147	39.62
Government Initiatives	128	34.50
Workload	94	25.34
Poor management	79	21.29
Paperwork	78	21.02
Stress	69	18.60
Pay	68	18.33
Long hours	52	14.02
Health	44	11.86
National Curriculum effects on children's motivation/lack of enjoyment	38	10.24

Workload, paperwork, long hours and pay are important disincentives that appear throughout the research literature. Pay is thought to be a main cause of wastage in early reports: the government has attempted to deal with this through changes in pay structures. The House of Commons Education and Skills Committee (2004) feel that pay is no longer the main issue in terms of retention. Our research indicates that although pay is an issue for some teachers (18%) it is not as important as it was.

Workload

Government has recognised that workload is a significant factor in teacher wastage and the new workload agreement came into force later in 2005. Nevertheless, workload and related issues such as paperwork and long hours remain important reasons for teachers leaving. For many women workload impinges on family responsibilities; for many men it compares less favourably with other occupations.

> The paper work – especially record keeping was too much. Four hours every Sunday on record keeping is too much to expect from a mother of young children – or any other experienced teacher for that matter. (Female primary ex-teacher)

Too much after hours work (planning/marking)/I have a far higher earning potential/I found teaching ...I was working every evening during the week and at least one day per weekend, whereas my friends in alternative jobs had much more free time out of normal working hours. (Male primary ex-teacher)

Pupil behaviour

Pupil behaviour is often mentioned before pay and is more frequently cited:

I know a number of ex-teachers – all have left the profession for the same reasons – poor discipline, no trust in teachers to get on and teach, and long hours. We were all exhausted. (Male secondary ex-teacher)

I may go abroad to teach and live in a different country where teaching is less stressful – especially the paper work (not necessary) and children are better behaved. (Male primary teacher)

Pupil behaviour affects teachers in London schools (Hutchings *et al*, 2000) and has became a common feature in research studies from 2003 onwards. Our respondents' comments suggest that they see this as a recent and growing phenomenon.

Behaviour becomes ever more challenging...I have enjoyed working with children, but find their attitudes to life and sense of irresponsibility ('It's not mine, It's not my fault') increasingly distressing. (Female primary teacher)

Most recently the House of Commons Education and Skills Committee (2004) recognised that pupil behaviour affects retention. They recommend that each LEA should have attendance and behaviour consultants and that behaviour improvement projects (BIPs) should be extended. They also note that action on pupil behaviour is supported by the behaviour and attendance strand of the Key Stage 3 Strategy (2003:25).

Government initiatives

Government initiatives are another important reason for leaving teaching (Table 1). The main issues mentioned are government interference, constant change, and unrealistic demands.

Too many experienced teachers have been driven out of teaching because of ill thought out government schemes, bureaucracy and target setting. In most cases these schemes are later found to have not worked. (Male secondary ex-teacher)

> Government always trying out new-fangled 'remedies' and not willing to tackle the root of the problem... Huge work overload caused by government initiatives and policies designed to make schools more accountable. (Female primary ex-teacher)

However, constant change and excessive demands due to government initiatives do not appear to feature as an area of concern in the government's own plans to improve recruitment and retention.

Poor management and stress

Poor management has been a recurring issue (Spear *et al*, 2000) and this has been recognised as an important factor in improving retention by the House of Commons Education and Skills Committee, (2004:32):

> We are not convinced, however, that training for the National Professional Qualification for Headship emphasises adequately that the way in which a headteacher manages a school can be decisive in persuading teachers to remain at that school. The impact of the retention of high quality staff on improvements in pupil achievement needs to be emphasised and good practice on retention issues needs to be explicitly included in the training.

Unfortunately management is equated with 'leadership' by this Committee who have put in place training for headteachers (NPQH) but do not encourage any specific management training for senior team or middle management within schools. Being poorly managed may well exasperate teachers' stress levels.

As noted above, stress is often mentioned by teachers as a reason for leaving the profession. In our survey 19 per cent of teachers cite stress as a reason for leaving. Work stress and related conditions are the second most commonly reported work related ill-health problems in Great Britain, with an estimated half a million people suffering from work-related stress, anxiety or depression (Health and Safety Executive, 2004). A survey by the helpline *Teacherline* (Earnshaw *et al*, 2002) found that more than two in five teachers in England and Wales have experienced major stress, mainly due to workload, in the past two years. *Teacherline* says that work stress in teachers is four times more prevalent than in industry (Bunting, 2000). The Health and Safety Executive (2000) observes that teachers and nurses have the highest prevalence of work-related stress, with 42 per cent of teachers and 23 per cent of those in other education and welfare roles reporting high levels of stress.

Mackay *et al* (2004) have identified six factors which are likely to affect stress levels: the demands of the job, the degree of control, the level of support, the nature of working relationships, role delineation and the management of change. Some of these reasons are given by teachers to explain why they leave the profession; the demands of the job and management of change are the most frequently reported reasons for leaving. Pupil behaviour – working relationships – is another source of stress. Management structure, style and ability, emerge as important factors affecting leaving as they are also causes of stress – level of support, working relationships and role delineation. So, although teachers' reasons for leaving are not always categorised as stress they are probably likely to be stress related.

The *Tackling Stress* booklet (NUT, 1999) lists the main causes of teacher stress[3]. When these are compared with the reasons given by teachers for leaving the profession, a close relationship is evident between the two. Only salary and personal circumstances cannot be linked directly with the NUT list, although it is established elsewhere (ACAS, 2004) that concerns about salary and personal circumstances can be causes of stress. Workplace bullying, which appears on the NUT list, does not feature in the literature concerned with retention and recruitment, although there are two brief references (Smithers and Robinson, 2005; MORI, 2002). Smithers and Robinson (2005:61) observe, as a result of in-depth interviews, that 'poor leadership perceived as bullying in some circumstances is a common thread in the comments on unhappiness with the old school'.

In a survey for the GTC by MORI in 2002 (MORI, 2002), amongst the possible responses to the question, 'Which three of the following, if any, demotivate you most as a teacher?' was 'Bullying by Head/ Management/Colleagues etc'. Of 70,000 replies, 4 per cent (all women) chose this response. This is a low percentage in the context of the survey and does not appear as an important factor in the final report, but this MORI survey covered all registered teachers, as opposed to potential leavers, and in this context reports of bullying as de-motivating might be important. Lack of reference to workplace bullying in the teacher wastage literature is noteworthy, given that 9 per cent of our sample offer it as a reason for leaving and that Hoel and Cooper (2000), found that teachers were amongst the highest profession at risk from bullying, with 15.5 per cent of teachers stating they were currently being bullied and 35.4 per cent that they had been bullied over the last five years. In addition, our survey finds that poor management, the second most commonly mentioned reason for leaving, is often linked with bullying and stress. The NASUWT (1996) finds that bullying comes mainly from those in positions of power, such as headteachers, deputy heads and heads of year/department, and that the biggest group of victims are women in their mid-forties.

Many of our teachers suggest reasons for leaving that can be attributed to poor management and be very stressful: bullying, health problems such as depression and breakdowns, workload and long hours particularly stand out. In our study far more primary teachers mention these reasons than mention poor management. The reverse is true at secondary level. It is possible that primary teachers, in a smaller close-knit community, feel too close to their management peers to attribute problems to them and instead speak of individual stress factors. Secondary teachers in larger schools are generally more removed from the senior management team: this may be the reason that they are more likely to attribute their stress factors directly to poor management.

Gender differences and stress

Smithers and Robinson (2003) observe that whereas men are more likely to resign because of school factors, women tend to cite personal reasons. We also find that more women give personal reasons for leaving (30% of women and 19% of men). If we also include responses under the heading 'other reasons', we find that 48 per cent of women and 40 per cent of men identify their reasons for leaving under these two headings. Poor management and bullying are referred to by men and women under the heading 'other reasons', although more men speak of poor management, and many women speak of workplace bullying. More women give stress, poor health, workload, long hours and bullying as reasons for leaving the profession. The Health and Safety Executive (2004) suggests that more women than men report their jobs to be stressful and we find that women more commonly cite stress as a reason for leaving teaching.

Reasons for leaving teaching appear complex. It is easier to make sense of them if it is recognised that all the reasons for leaving outlined in Table 3 are in fact stress factors, and that teachers are choosing to represent their stresses using different labels. These different labels for potentially similar and connected experiences in teaching may reflect gender differences in the responses: men teachers, like men trainees (chapter 6), may seek to save face by denying or re-labelling personal difficulties, such as stress or bullying, which are

Table 3: Management/stress related reasons for leaving, by gender

	men (N=129)		women (N=233)	
	n	%	n	%
Poor management	30	23.26	49	21.03
Paperwork	30	23.26	48	20.60
Workload	20	15.50	73	31.33
Long hours	13	10.08	39	16.74
Stress	13	10.08	56	24.03
Bullying	10	7.75	21	9.01
Health	8	6.20	36	15.45
Low morale	7	5.43	22	9.44
Racism/unfairness	1	0.78	6	2.58

un-masculine. Poor management and paperwork are more objective reasons for leaving than stress and it may be that women can acknowledge more easily than men that they are being bullied.

Other gender differences

There is relatively little difference between men and women regarding work, pay and conditions as reasons for leaving but when government initiatives are also considered, since these relate directly to school conditions, there is no difference. However, men are more likely to consider leaving the profession because of poor pupil discipline. Powney *et al* (2003), and MORI (2002) observe that men are significantly more de-motivated than female teachers by pupil behaviour. We have found similar gender differences. Almost 46 per cent of men compared with 37 per cent of women cite poor pupil behaviour as the reason they are leaving (Table 4).

Government initiatives are the second most important reason for leaving, given by slightly more men than women. Men also refer more to management and paperwork. Taken together, these three reasons (pupil behaviour, government initiatives and management), link closely with issues of power and control and indicate that men are more concerned about this than women.

Powney *et al* (2003) find that men are more likely than women to want to leave for higher pay and more opportunities and observe that men, particularly younger men, are more likely to have considered leaving because pay is too low, or to seek better opportunities elsewhere. MORI (2002) observes that men are significantly less likely to

Table 4: Top ten reasons given for leaving the teaching profession, by gender

Reason for leaving	Number of of male teachers	% of male teachers	Number of female teachers	% of female teachers
Pupil behaviour	59	45.74	87	37.34
Government Initiatives	47	36.43	80	34.33
Workload	20	15.50	73	31.33
Stress	13	10.08	56	24.03
Poor management	30	23.26	49	21.03
Paperwork	30	23.26	48	20.60
Pay	22	17.05	46	19.74
Long hours	13	10.08	39	16.74
Health	8	6.20	36	15.45
National Curriculum effects on children's motivation/lack of enjoyment	14	10.85	24	10.30

think they will still be a teacher in five years' time. In our survey there is very little difference overall between men and women regarding pay as a reason for leaving but slightly more women than men (20% as opposed to 17%) give this as one reason for leaving.

Gender differences by phase of schooling look somewhat different. For men in primary schools pay is more often mentioned than by women (31% as opposed to 16%) as a reason for leaving, but at secondary level the reverse is found (11% as opposed 25%). For men this may reflect the lower salaries and fewer promotion opportunities in primary schools and for women the disproportionate occupation of management roles by men in secondary schools.

One of the reasons given by government, parents and governors and also by many teachers for recruiting more male teachers is that they will have a positive effect on pupil behaviour, yet our own work and that of others (Powney et al, 2003) suggests that men are more likely than women to leave teaching because of poor pupil behaviour.

Although the numbers are small, reports of workplace bullying as a reason for leaving are of great concern. Bullying and lack of support are always mentioned in the context of senior management, but not always the headteacher. The government is putting management training in place for headteachers but there does not appear to be any initiative for the training of middle managers; such a move might reduce poor management and reduce bullying by managers. Although reported by both men and women, bullying and stress are identified as a problem by more women than men. While the NASUWT (1996) report women teachers to be the major victims of bullying, our data suggest that it is an issue for men too (Table 2).

Destinations

As Figure 2 shows, many teachers move to other teaching jobs, a number of women teachers leave to have babies and there are also a large numbers of retirements each year. The number leaving to take other jobs has risen steadily since 1993.

Destinations include supply work (primary 23%, secondary 9%), jobs in education that do not involve teaching in schools (primary 12%, secondary 15%), and jobs outside education (primary 13%, secondary 16%). Primary teachers also leave to look after their families (11%), and secondary teachers for travel breaks (8%) and

Figure 2: Destinations of full-time permanent resigning teachers (1987-2003)

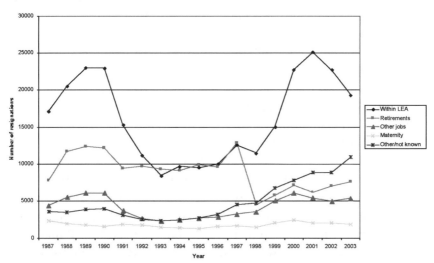

Source: Employers Organisation 2004

other career breaks (8%). About half of those leaving the profession to work elsewhere move into education-related posts, and the GTC (Ross and Hutchings, 2003) has suggested that the number of such posts, which often require teaching experience, has increased in recent years.

Figures provided by Smithers and Robinson (2005) show that from 2002 to 2004, fewer teachers in primary schools are taking other education posts on resignation, and more are taking alternative employment. Resignations for maternity are far more common among primary teachers but retirements are very similar for primary and secondary. An examination of figures taken from Robinson and Smithers (2005) shows that more men than women primary teachers leave to take up other jobs and to travel, and that more men than women secondary teachers take early retirement (Table 5).

Five women in our survey, but no men, left for reasons of maternity and family care. There are a number of retirements but most of these are early or ill health retirements (only two normal retirements) suggesting that only those who have actively chosen to leave have been motivated to complete this questionnaire. A small number are taking career breaks and expect to return to teaching at some later date, but the majority have taken up alternative employment (45% of women and 41% of men). Very few of these jobs involve teaching in schools or tutorial work; just five men and eleven women are doing supply work or private tuition. A considerable number of those who took alternative employment say that nothing will induce them to return to teaching – as these typical extracts in response to the question: 'If you are leaving the teaching profession do you envisage returning to it at some point in the future?' show:

> No. I could not face it! The exhaustion and the level of conflict are much greater than when I started teaching. The job is having a detrimental effect on my health and lifestyle. (Female secondary teacher, about to leave)

> No. Pay, target mania, bullying management. (Male primary ex-teacher)

> No. Too much bureaucracy, rubbish pay, disruptive children, bullying headmaster. (Female primary ex-teacher)

> No. Wild horses wouldn't drag me – I like my sanity! (Male secondary ex-teacher)

The majority of those who have left are definite that they will not return to teaching under any circumstances and many of those

Table 5: Destinations of classroom teachers by gender (2004)

Destination Per Cent	Primary		Secondary	
	Male	Female	Male	Female
All teaching employment	67.7	59.8	65.1	65.8
Other Employment	5.7	4.2	4.6	5.5
Family Care	0.0	4.0	0.5	3.6
Travel	5.7	3.1	2.8	3.9
Overseas Return Home	0.0	0.2	0.7	0.2
Normal-Age Retirement	3.8	5.6	4.6	3.9
Ill Health Retirement	0.0	1.9	2.5	1.6
Early Retirement	10.5	11.0	7.6	4.9
Redundancy	0.0	0.2	0.3	0.0
Other	3.8	5.2	3.8	3.9
Not Known	2.9	4.9	7.4	6.7

i. Maternity excluded. ii. Gender not recorded for one primary teacher and 13 secondary teachers.

Source: Smithers and Robinson, 2005

about to leave indicate that they will consider any work rather than continue teaching. However, some say that they might possibly return if circumstances change:

> Being a teacher is almost like having two jobs. Your job in the classroom and your job in the evenings and at weekends preparing plans and maintaining records. If much more non-contact time was offered, or overtime pay for the extra hours worked. (Male primary ex-teacher)

> More support for teachers to help prevent stress and anxiety building up to the point that it becomes a problem. Also better help when/if it does. (Female secondary ex-teacher)

> *Far* less unnecessary paperwork and petty political correctness. Let the teacher teach! (Male secondary ex-teacher)

What happens to intrinsic motivation?

Much research (see chapter 4) refers to the intrinsic motivation of student teachers to teach. They become teachers because they like working with children, they want to help them learn and they want to make a difference to young lives. However, more than 10 per cent of our surveyed teachers admit sadly that the effects of the NC on children and the loss of enjoyment in teaching are reasons for their leaving.

> The National Curriculum has taken the joy out of teaching... Obsession with results has placed the onus on the teacher, removing from the student the need to motivate themselves. The National Curriculum is demanding to the degree it negates spontaneity, and makes it difficult to make learning matter relevant. (Male secondary teacher, about to leave)

> Glad to see that creativity is now getting more emphasis but still think that that SATs and Ofsteds are draining the energy of teachers. Teachers want to teach, want enthusiastic children, want to be inspirational, want children to achieve – why else would we do the job... Better management and motivational methods need to be used to encourage and inspire teachers. (Female primary ex-teacher)

If problems regarding deteriorating pupil behaviour – cited by 40 per cent of our leavers – which also undermines intrinsic reasons for teaching in the first place are also taken into consideration, it becomes clear that tinkering with pay and conditions is not going to resolve the problem of wastage from teaching.

Although such comments are made by both men and women, the men apart from two are from secondary schools, and the women, all except eight, are from primary schools. This suggests that the intrinsic rewards of teaching (Reid and Thornton, 2000) although important to the vast majority of trainee teachers, and a key recruitment motivator, remain more important for women than men in primary schools at least, even when they are considering getting out of the profession, and may be key factors for wanting to get out. If the reasons you became a teacher are removed, improved pay and conditions are unlikely to make you want to stay, no matter how good government's intentions might be. However, at all stages of teaching, pay and conditions have greater impact on men than on women.

Conclusions

Men are more likely than women to leave teaching for higher pay and better opportunities elsewhere (Powney *et al*, 2003) and our survey of leavers shows that for primary school teachers pay is more often mentioned as a reason for leaving by men than by women.

Male teachers, particularly male primary teachers, have a choice of better paid options open to them (see chapter 3). If pay and conditions do not match the workload involved, if status remains low, if central control and direction remains intense, and if reasons for teaching in the first place are removed then we should not be surprised that so many teachers are leaving or that men, especially male primary teachers, are disproportionate amongst them.

Recommended reading

Ross, A. and Hutchings, M. (2003). *Attracting, Developing and Retaining Effective Teachers in the United Kingdom of Great Britain and Northern Ireland.* OECD Country Background Report. London: Institute for Policy Studies in Education, London Metropolitan University

Powney, J. Wilson, V. Hall, S. Davidson, J. Kirk, S. Edward, S with Mirza, H.S. (2003) *Teachers' Careers: the Impact of Age, Disability, Ethnicity, Gender and Sexual Orientation.* The Scottish Council for Research in Education Research Report No 488

9

Contradictions and Constraints

Introduction

Teaching and the division of labour within it cannot be understood in isolation from the complex and changing social world in which it is located. Teachers do not exist in a social vacuum. Gender, power and status issues inevitably permeate their work and their social worlds, whether they want them to or not. The roles, responsibilities and career paths they adopt are an outcome of politically and socially structured possibilities that in part reflect and result from gendered relationships of domination and subordination in society.

Sargent (2000:430) says that

> ... we need to conceptualise the low participation of men in women's work in terms of the structural impediments that exist from the perspective of the men who might choose to cross over.

Our research has explored the perspectives of men in education alongside their low participation rates and possible explanations for this. Structural impediments have changed over time; some of these are cultural and implicit rather than formally inscribed in codes and prohibitions but this does not make them any less inhibiting for men wishing to 'cross over'.

Expectations regarding working in education with children have changed during the past 100 years. Where once teaching was regarded as a respectable, reasonably high status occupation, a masculine profession involving intellectual work and material rewards, its current low status within the labour market and its relatively low salary make it an unlikely choice for high aspiring or hegemonically masculine men.

When men take this pathway they do disproportionately well. Whether in education or elsewhere, men are more likely to seek and achieve promotion, higher salaries and higher status positions than women, and structural features of society, such as patriarchy, continue to facilitate this. Senior positions in education continue to reflect the traditional breadwinner status of men and stereotypical male/female roles in the labour market. Cultural impediments to men teaching are less pervasive at this level. Men managing women fits better with social expectations.

Rhetoric and reality

Current perceptions of its lowly status and as a feminine domain make teaching a difficult occupational choice for many men. Family, friends, teachers and careers advisers often have different ideas about suitable jobs for them. Add to this the more recent concerns, about child abuse and paedophilia, and a new focus on men and masculinities and the cultural barriers for men choosing to teach become even stronger. It takes considerable strength and determination to challenge and overcome spoken and unspoken public questioning of their motives and sexualities.

TDA and government attempts to increase the numbers of men in teaching rely on stereotypical masculine images and characteristics, and by omission effectively contrast these negatively with typical notions of the feminine. Rather than child-centredness, professional care, sensitivity, commitment, tough but worthy work and a nurturing role, potential male recruits are enticed in with masculine stereotypes that emphasise sport and athleticism, intellectual stimulation and challenge, tough but rewarding work, respect and leadership possibilities. Socially framed perceptions and expectations of teaching as feminised are overtly contradicted. Neither of these stereotypes are attractive: the first is insulting to men and the second is insulting to women.

Social structures help shape and form our occupational choices but they do not determine them. Men who teach are not a homogeneous group. They occupy a range of masculinities which, whilst shaped by social structures, are constantly negotiated and re-made during the course of their training and careers. Men who become teachers will, and should, present a variety of masculinities to their pupils.

Missed men?

There are certainly fewer men teaching now than ever before but once in teaching men are not missed from management and leadership positions. Their tendency to show greater concern for higher pay and status is disproportionately met by a glass escalator that facilitates the career development of those men who seek it. By exploiting this advantage some men are complicit in the maintenance of hegemonic masculinity (Connell, 1995), patriarchy and even misogyny, despite incidences where their own masculine identity does not conform to such stereotypes. It is a gendered privilege that is rarely challenged even by those men who recognise its existence, and many do not.

A recent *TES* editorial (Opinion, 2002:22) suggested that the dearth of men teachers, which results in the education of children by women, 'damages children's education, equal opportunities, and society in general'. The evidence available does not support this view. The quality of teaching and learning in education is of the utmost importance but it does not hinge upon the gender of teachers. While there are amazingly few studies exploring the differential impact men and women teachers *might* have on children's learning, those that do exist (Bricheno and Thornton, 2002; Carrington and Tymms, 2005) find no discernable differences. Despite assertions to the contrary, the presence of men teachers appears to have no direct or significant impact on boys' attitudes to school, their behaviour or their academic achievements. What matters is not teacher gender but teacher quality, alongside the degree of social advantage and disadvantage of the pupils concerned. There is no substance to support popular assertions that more men teachers will improve boys' behaviour and achievement in schools.

Missing men?

There has undoubtedly been a relative and fairly recent decline in the proportion of men teachers, but it has not been as dramatic as public panics suggest. As noted in chapter 3, in primary schools we have moved gradually from a high of 29 per cent men in 1938 to a low of 16 per cent in 2004, whilst the proportion of men headteachers is almost the same now as it was 100 years ago. The decline of male teachers in secondary schools is much less noticeable, falling from 55 to just below 50 per cent between 1962 and 2004.

Nevertheless, men are increasingly missing from education, particularly from primary schools, and we have identified some of the reasons why this might be so: relative to other graduate careers pay has been eroded, status is low, and social structures and cultural expectations work against men entering predominantly female occupations such as teaching, whether they are actually feminised in practice or not. Men who teach are vulnerable to accusations of child abuse and homosexuality; a climate of suspicion surrounds them. They must find ways in which to integrate and function effectively within a predominantly female domain; this frequently involves adopting stereotypically masculine activities within schools, such as leading sport or taking on IT responsibilities.

Men are in contradictory positions in teaching. At entry level they stand out, are marginalised and decentred. In this predominantly female environment and at this stage in their careers they are on the periphery. They are at the same time a valuable and rare commodity yet deemed to have suspect motives or sexual orientations. Expectations of them are both conflicting and stereotypical. Their personal aspirations may be equally contradictory; intrinsic motivations for entering teaching contrast sharply with opportunities for higher status and greater influence through rapid promotion once they are in.

Morale is low, public attitudes generally to teachers as a workforce are ambivalent and pay is an issue, particularly for men. Our respondents from the Men's Club believe that men are generally attracted to high status, highly paid jobs. Teaching is neither, but they envisage rapid promotion, as men, to more highly paid positions: a factor in teaching that has been evidenced by a number of studies (Reid and Thornton, 2000; Thornton and Bricheno, 2000; Lynch, 1994; Warren, 1997).

Where good pay and high status is not forthcoming men are more likely than women to leave teaching. This is especially so for primary school teachers where higher pay and promotion opportunities are more limited and better paid options outside teaching are open to them. If pay and conditions do not match the workload involved, if the status of teaching remains low, if central control and direction remains intense, and if reasons for teaching in the first place are erased such as enjoyment and intrinsic worthwhileness, we should not be surprised that so many teachers leave or that men, especially male primary teachers, are disproportionate amongst them.

Men may be missing from education but it cannot reasonably be claimed that this relative and definitely recent decline in their numbers has actually *caused* education to become feminised or *caused* poorer behaviour amongst boys. Nor are missing men responsible for boys' current, relative and recent underachievement when compared to girls'. We can find no reliable evidence to support such claims or the public panics that surround them.

Men as a group have consistently entered teaching with lower qualifications than women as HEIs find themselves under pressure from the TTA to recruit more men from the small pool of available applicants. Those entering with lower qualifications are less likely to complete their course, thus wasting valuable resources. Raising entrance requirements could work against government efforts to recruit more men. But it may also work to attract different groups of men, perhaps those with higher school leaving qualifications and who are more usually associated with middle-class rather than working-class origins. That might enhance completion rates for men on ITE courses but at the same time potentially restrict an upward mobility opportunity for working-class men with lower levels of educational qualifications who are interested in teaching. Too firm an adherence to higher entry qualifications might also inhibit access to teaching for career-changing mature men who are an important pool of potential recruits and who have demonstrated a greater propensity to cross gendered occupational boundaries successfully.

Ultimately we must recruit high calibre male – and female – students for the right reasons, such as a commitment to quality education and the potential ability to teach well. We could, but should not, recruit more men on the basis of skewed career advantage seemingly derived from the mere fact of being male. To be successful in raising male recruitment the whole profession of teaching, and primary teaching in particular, needs raised status and improved financial reward.

A masculinised profession?

Claims that teaching has become feminised may be a major impediment to recruiting more men (Carrington, 2002: 301) but such assertions hinge upon a negative interpretation of all things feminine, and there are now counterclaims that teaching is becoming 'masculinised' (Arnot and Miles, 2005). How should we interpret these claims?

We accept that teaching has long been, and remains, a predominantly female occupation in the UK, but does that necessarily equate to a feminised profession? Teaching, especially primary teaching, is almost always constructed as feminised because of the disproportionate number of women teachers and also because it is often assumed that the work of teachers, especially primary teachers, must be founded on stereotypical feminine traits, such as caring for, rather than about, children, and mothering skills.

We are certainly not the first researchers to recognise an increasing trend towards the masculinisation of education (Mahony *et al*, 2004a; Skelton, 2002). Centralised controls and interventions are numerous and seemingly unending early in the 21st century, yet it was not long ago that Lawton (1982) talked of the *Secret Garden of the Curriculum*. In his famous Ruskin College speech in 1976 James Callaghan (1976) opened this *secret garden* to public scrutiny, enabling political interference in matters hitherto left to teachers. It was the beginning of a process that led inexorably towards the ERA in 1988; before this the curriculum was nominally decided by school governors but more usually left up to the headteacher. After the ERA, control of the curriculum, and to some extent pedagogy, was removed from teachers. We would not want to see a return to such *secrets* but we would advocate professional direction to, and control of, what goes on in our schools.

Following the ERA (DES, 1989), the ethos of education, its pedagogies, curriculum and assessment have changed substantially. Education has become increasingly masculine in orientation, in terms of its formal structures, such as

■ the management of teachers' roles and practises

■ the appraisal of teachers, competitive league tables and targets, performance related pay

■ central control over the curriculum and pedagogy

■ an increased emphasis on subject specialisms, especially in primary schools, and

■ extended internal hierarchies in what was once a fairly flat management structure even in secondary schools.

Is this a masculinisation of education? For the classroom teacher the reduction in autonomy and a prescriptive curriculum which must be adhered to smacks of passivity: a stereotypically female attribute. Perhaps, at this level teaching is being feminised, not because the workforce is predominantly female, but because teachers at the chalk face have lost control of their work.

The role of headteacher increasingly emphasises management and administration rather than personal teaching excellence and leading others by example and it is accompanied by greatly increased administrative workloads. In many ways this emphasis fits a stereo-typically masculine view of leadership in other work environments more closely and contrasts sharply with feminine care and nurtur-ing. Teaching is now highly structured and controlled, planned, organised, managed and evaluated largely in accord with hege-monic male preferences but contrary to perceived women's pre-ferences (Mahony *et al*, 2004a). The more recent emphasis on testing and assessment, performance indicators, hierarchical management and administrative structures moves teaching as an occupation into a stereotypically male domain.

Given these increasingly masculine characteristics men might be expected to turn to teaching in greater numbers, and yet here is another contradiction; the masculinised job of headteacher is ap-parently being rejected by men and taken up by women. Teaching appears to provide women with more opportunity to gain manage-ment positions (Wylie, 2000). As the proportion of female headships gradually increases: we may ask: are women now more attracted to this role or are men increasingly rejecting this role? Ross (cited in Budge, 1999) suggests that, given these changes, perhaps men no longer see headship as the career opportunity that it once was. The current large number of unfilled headteacher positions (Hastings, 2005) suggests that teachers, both male and female, are rejecting this increasingly bureaucratic and administrative role.

Most men and women enter teaching for altruistic reasons, wanting to work with children and seeing it as a challenging and rewarding career. Neither would seem likely to aspire to an increasingly passive and externally controlled occupation. Teachers' reasons for leaving show their dislike for increasing bureaucracy and administrative requirements, the constant interference by government and their distress about their lack of power over the curriculum.

In the meantime women remain the front line workers in our schools. As a so-called semi- profession they are deemed in need of control (see chapter 4), and in the current educational environment this will be through centralised bureaucratic controls. Men in cen-trally powerful roles in government can manage this without need-ing to be physically at the chalk face, in schools and classrooms. Direction and control is what really matters in education and that is where the power lies.

In the context of power and control we turn to the issue of centrality which we discussed in chapter 2. The concepts of centrality and social integration help us to understand the contradiction between both the lack of men in teaching and their occupation of positions of power and authority within it. Men generally occupy more powerful positions in society than women. The lack of power and influence of male classroom teachers is obvious. At this level men generally don't have power. Here they are de-centred, stripped of the societal and personal expectations of power conferred on them by hegemonic notions of masculinity. In the past, substantial power and influence, increased centrality, was obtained by becoming a headteacher. But now that control and power over the substance of education is largely in the hands of politicians and quangos, this route to centrality and greater influence over education is not as inviting as it once was. If men seek to become headteachers to reinforce their masculinity, their reduced power over the curriculum and pedagogy is a barrier. Is the increasingly masculinised and newly-formed managerialist and administrative role of the headteacher going to be a sufficient attraction?

Teaching is becoming masculinised in terms of stereotypically male working environments although not in ways that appeal to the type of men who up until now have become teachers. It is possible that men who enter teaching in the future will do so for the status of managerial and administrative functions, rather than the altruistic reasons given by the teachers we have talked to. This could result in an American style split between school administration and teaching, a new two-tier system of school leadership. It is certainly possible that within the changing environment of education and teaching that quite different types of men and women will be attracted to it: those stereotypical men who might want to be administrators and managers and those – stereotypically women – who are judged fit to be technicians, deliverers of pre-packaged curricula according to centrally prescribed methods. It is not possible to predict whether this will or will not enhance the quality of teaching in our schools.

Political control of the curriculum and a masculinisation of teaching roles and functions has not so far attracted more men to the profession. However, there are signs that central control of the curriculum is now loosening and Ofsted inspections being toned down. The GTC may yet provide the teaching profession with some degree of autonomy over its work. Perhaps in the future we will see more men – and women – wanting to join a profession in which the intrinsic rewards outweigh bureaucratic disincentives.

Conclusions

Teaching has the potential, yet to be realised, to become a male-dominated profession. We are unsure where this leaves women teachers. Despite claims of feminisation women teachers are currently operating and working well in this masculinised educational environment (Woods and Carlyle, 2002). Under increasingly female tutelage educational achievements have risen dramatically, even if some boys have not yet reached the level achieved by some girls. This is a success story for women teachers that is not acknowledged sufficiently, masked by vociferous concerns about male absence.

That some men reject rather than lay claim to the newer, masculinised styles of management, audit and prescribed content in teaching does not mean that it does not work in their favour. New groups of male teachers, from different origins and with different orientations may well be attracted to teaching as a career, especially if the financial incentives remain good and a more realistic view of what teaching actually entails is available to them.

Men as teachers are in a good position to challenge traditional gender stereotypes: we wish they would. A diverse teaching force is desirable but positive discrimination towards men is not. Quality teachers are the major requirement. The door is increasingly open to men. Will they walk through?

Notes

1 TheTTA (TeacherTraining Agency) was renamed theTDA (Teacher Development Agency) in Summer 2005. Within the text we have used the appropriate name (TTA orTDA) for the date of the discussion of publication.

2 Schools began teaching the General Certificate of Secondary Education, or GCSE, in autumn 1986, with the first pupils sitting the exam in 1988. Under the old 'O' level and CSE system, grades were awarded primarily according to statistical rules which measured each candidate's performance relatively against those of competing candidates (Norm referencing).The introduction of the GCSE meant that, for the first time, grades would be allocated with reference to absolute standards of knowledge, understanding and skill (Criterion referencing).

3 CAUSES OFTEACHER STRESS (NUT, 1999)

Excessive working hours

Risk of violence from pupils, parents and intruders

Excessive workload

Lack of support with bureaucracy, form filling and routine tasks

Rising class sizes

Lack of job security due to redundancy and fixed term contracts

Pupil misbehaviour

Lack of control over the job

Burden of providing cover

Changes to assessment and testing requirements

Poor management

Pressures due to Ofsted inspection

Workplace bullying

Threat to early retirement arrangements

Crumbling schools

Disparagement of profession by politicians and media

Lack of public esteem

Changes in curriculum and courses

4 For example, teaching, for men, was characteristically a life-long career with a salary about 20% higher than that of women, who were expected to resign their posts upon marriage. However, the McNair report (1944) and the Equal Pay Act of 1970 meant that women could also view teaching as a permanent career, and expect salaries in parity with those of men.

Appendix:
Details of research

A1. Subject specialism in primary schools

Dates: 1988 – 1990

Sample: 85 interviews with all headteachers and class teachers, 63 classes in 22 primary schools, in one education division in South West Hertfordshire.

Methods: Interviews were conducted with all headteachers and class teachers in the sample (a total of 85), and 63 teachers' classrooms were observed in action. An equal number of reception, year 2, year 3 and year 6 classes were studied in order to gauge any differences between curriculum organisation and practice in key stage 1 and key stage 2.

Further sources of information:

Thornton, M. (1996) Subject Specialism, Gender and Status: The Example of Primary School Mathematics, *Education 3-13*, Vol.24, No.3, pp.53-54

Thornton, M. (1992) Unpublished PhD, University of London Institute of Education, 'Subject Specialism and the Primary School Curriculum'

A2. Men into primary teaching: Who goes where?

Dates: 1995-8

Sample: From a sample of 390 schools, 220 schools located within a 25 mile radius of Watford responded, across several LEAs (56.4% response rate); Headteachers provided information covering a total of 1872 teachers in their schools.

Methods: Questionnaire completed by headteachers, seeking information about staff gender, curriculum responsibilities, seniority, position on pay scales and age range taught.

Further sources of information:

Thornton, M. (1999a), 'Men into primary teaching: Who goes where? Dilemmas of entry, survival and career prospects', *Education 3-13*, June, pp. 50-56

Thornton M. (1996) 6th International Conference, Centre for Educational Development, Appraisal and Research (CEDAR), March, University of Warwick: Subject Specialism, Gender and Status: The Example of Primary School Mathematics

A3. Male B Ed perceptions

Dates: 1997

Sample: Male BEd students from one University at the end of their first and fourth years in 1997; 5 of the 13 first year males completed the questionnaire and 3 of them also agreed to be interviewed; 3 of the 7 fourth year males completed the questionnaire and all agreed to be interviewed.

Methods: Open-ended questionnaires to all BEd students in first and fourth years plus an invitation to 'talk further' through a follow-up interview. Analysis of the text and transcriptions focused on the key issues emerging from the interviews and questionnaires.

Further sources of information:

Thornton, M. (2000) Male Students on Primary Initial Teacher Education Courses, in S. Shah, (Ed.) pp.70-84, *Equality Issues for the New Millennium*, Aldershot: Ashgate Press.

A4. Men's Club

Dates:1997-1998

Sample: Twelve of a possible 25 male students on a four year teacher training course at one English university attended the Men's Club during 1997/8. Ten of these students also completed questionnaires about their experience of ITT and 9 took part in individual in-depth interviews.

Methods: A club was established for male students training to be primary school teachers as an attempt to address the issue of high wastage rates amongst male students. Field notes, interviews and a questionnaire survey of volunteer male students, not all of whom attended the club, enabled identification of key features relating to: their training course, general perceptions of their chosen career, and the success and failure rates amongst these male students.

Further sources of information:

Thornton, M. (1999b), Reducing Wastage among Men Student Teachers in Primary Courses: a male club approach, *Journal of Education for Teaching*, 25:1, pp. 41-53

A5. Teachers' careers

Dates: 1998

Sample: 207 respondents (27 males and 180 females) completed questionnaire and 54 follow up interviews were conducted (9 males and 45 females)

Methods: A random, representative sample of primary schools in England and Wales was surveyed using a questionnaire in two parts: factual questions such as age and qualifications of teachers, followed by a free-response section. Text analysis of free-response data from part two explored the reasons reported by teachers for their promotion or lack of promotion and their views about seeking promotion. Open-ended, focused interviews were undertaken with selected respondents to explore informants' individual and personal responses to primary teaching as a career. Issues connected with teachers' career aspirations and their perceptions of beneficial or detrimental effects on these aspirations were also addressed in the interviews.

Further sources of information:

Thornton, M. and Bricheno, P. (2000), Primary Teachers Careers in England and Wales: the relationship between gender, role, position and promotion aspirations, in *Pedagogy, Culture and Society* Vol. 8, No.2, pp.187-206

A6. Students' reasons for choosing primary teaching as a career

Dates: 1998-1999

Sample: 1611 first year undergraduates and PGCE primary students across four chartered and seven non-chartered universities, plus three university colleges in England completed questionnaires and 148 were involved in follow-up interviews.

The institutional sample was broadly representative of the HEI training providers in England and the gender sample for both the questionnaire survey and the interviews was very close to the current intake figures of approximately 15 per cent male, 85% female

Methods: Questionnaires followed by interviews with a sample of those surveyed.

Further sources of information:

Thornton, M and Reid, I. (2001) Primary Teacher Recruitment: Careers Guidance and Advice, in *Education 3 -13*, Vol.29, No.2. pp 49-54

Thornton, M., Bricheno, P. and Reid, I. (2002) Students' reasons for wanting to teach in primary school, *Research in Education*, 67, p33-43

Reid, I and Thornton, M. (2000) *Students' Reasons for Choosing Primary School Teaching as a Career*, Centre for Equality Issues in Education, University of Hertfordshire, England.

A7. Staff gender balance

Dates: 2000-2001

Sample: 846 of 1,000 schools (85% of the sample).

Methods: An e-mail and telephone survey of a stratified representative sample of schools across England and Wales, combined with data from Ofsted reports and DfES statistics for these schools.

Further sources of information:

Bricheno, P. and Thornton, M. (2002) Staff Gender Balance in Primary Schools, *Research in Education*, 68, pp. 57-64

A8. Studies of drop-out

■ **Matched sample Natural Selection Longitudinal Study**

Dates: 1998- 2001

Sample: 42 male and 42 females Undergraduate ITE students from one English University.

Methods: Since 1995 the progress of all 42 male undergraduate ITE students at one university has been tracked, along with that of a matched group of female students at the same university. Students' qualifications, age on entry, subject specialisation and assessments at selection interviews were initially matched, and progress was monitored through the university's end of year assessments. The study examined the details of the records of these students over the whole of the time period October 1995 to June 2001.

■ **Student drop-out cohort study**

Dates conducted: 2001-2002

Sample: Data from 660 female and 978 male students joining four different programmes in one English University between 1996 and 1998.

Methods: data for withdrawal/failure rates of the full cohorts of students from four programmes within one English university were compared, for the period 1996 to 2002. The programmes chosen were: Education, Business Studies, Computer Science and Aerospace Engineering. The degree programmes were chosen for their vocational aspects and their gender balance: one course where the gender balance was similar (Business Studies) two where there were lower proportions of women (Aerospace Engineering and Computer Science). All these were four year courses and included a year's work placement.

Further sources of information:

Bricheno, P. and Thornton, M. (2003) Natural selection? Centrality, the selection process and their implications for male and female undergraduates on a primary initial teacher education course, paper presented at BERA 3rd September 2003, Heriot Watt University, Edinburgh

A9. Role models

Dates: 2003

Sample: 397 pupils (197 boys and 182 girls aged from 10 to 16 years) from four schools in Hertfordshire.

Methods: A questionnaire was administered to all pupils present on the day in years 5 and 6 of the primary and junior schools, and to all pupils in two classes each from Years 9 and 11 in the two secondary schools.

Further sources of information:

Bricheno, P. and Thornton, M. (2003) Role model, hero or champion? Children's views about role models, paper presented at BERA 3rd September 2003, Heriot Watt University, Edinburgh

Bricheno, P. and Thornton, M. (2005) Role model research revisited, paper presented at EERA, 7th September 2005, University College Dublin

A10. Leaving teaching

Dates: 2005

Sample: 371 teachers and ex-teachers

Methods: Advertisements in newspapers or magazines were used to invite teachers who have already left or who were about to leave the profession to complete an on-line survey. The questionnaire provided opportunities to write as much as desired in response to questions about reasons for leaving and destinations. Analysis of text focused on reasons for leaving and destinations. The first section provided face data such as sex, age and education sector last taught in.

Further sources of information: Papers will submitted to BERA and EERA 2006.

References

Aaronovitch, D. Are we just jealous of Wayne's world? *Observer*, 17th April 2005, p29

Abbott, D. (2002) Teachers are failing black boys, *Observer*, 6th January 2002, http://www.observer.co.uk/

ACAS (2004) *Stress at Work, Advisory Booklet*, last printed version: November 2004, last updated web version: November 2004, http://www.acas.org.uk/publications/B18.html

Acker, S. (1994) *Gendered Education*. Buckinghamshire: Open University Press

Alexander, R. (1984) *Primary Teaching*. London: Holt, Rinehart and Winston

Alexander, R. (1991) *Primary Education in Leeds: Twelfth and Final Report from the Primary Needs Independent Evaluation Project*. Leeds: University of Leeds

Alexander, R., Rose, J. and Woodhead, C. (1992) *Curriculum Organisation and Classroom Practice in Primary Schools: A Discussion Paper*. London: DES

Al-Khalifa, E. (1989) Management training and equal opportunities. NUT *Educational Review*, 3 (2): pp54-58

Allan, J. (1993) Male elementary teachers: Experiences and Perspectives, pp113-127 in C. L. Williams (Ed) *Doing 'Women's Work': Men in Non-traditional Occupations* . London: Sage.

Allan, J. (1994) *Anomaly as exemplar: The meanings of role-modeling for men elementary teachers*. Dubuque: Tri-College Department of Education (Eric Reproduction Service No. ED 378 190)

Apple, M. (1990) *Ideology and the Curriculum*, London: Routledge

Arnot, M., David, M. and Weiner, G (1996) *Educational Reforms and Gender Equality in Schools*. Manchester: Equal Opportunities Commission, Research Discussion Series No. 17

Arnot, M., David, M. and Weiner, G. (1999) *Closing the Gender Gap: Postwar Education and Social Change*. Cambridge: Polity Press

Arnot, M., Gray, J., James, M. and Rudduck, J. with Duveen, G., (1998) *A Review of Recent Research on Gender and Educational Performance*. Ofsted Research Series, London: The Stationery Office

Arnot, M. and Miles, P. (2005). A reconstruction of the gender agenda: the contradictory gender dimensions in New Labour's educational and economic policy. *Oxford Review of Education*, 31(1 Special Issue): pp173-189

Arnot, M., and Phipps, A. (2003). Gender and Education in the UK. Background paper for the UNESCO Global Monitoring Report *Education for All: the Leap to Equality*, http://www.efareport.unesco.org/

Ashley, M. and Lee, J. (2003) *Women Teaching Boys*. Stoke-on-Trent: Trentham Books

Askew, S. and Ross, C. (1988) *Boys Don't Cry: Boys and Sexism in Education*. Buckingham: Open University Press

Bagley, C. A. (1993) *Governor Training and Equal Opportunities*, NFER, Berkshire

Bandura, A. (1986) *Social Foundations of Thought and Action: A Social Cognitive Theory*. Englewood Cliffs, NJ, USA : Prentice-Hall

Barmby, P. and Coe, R. (2004) Recruiting and Retaining Teachers: Findings from Recent Studies Curriculum, Evaluation and Management Centre University of Durham, a paper presented at the British Educational Research Association Conference, Manchester, 14th – 18th September 2004

Barnard, N. (2000) Training salary lures men into classrooms, *Times Educational Supplement*, 19 th May 2000, p8

Baron-Cohen, S. (2003) *The Essential Difference: men, women and the extreme male brain*. London: Allen Lane Science.

Barret, F. J. (2001) The Organizational Construction of Hegemonic Masculinity: The Case of the US Navy, in S. M. Whitehead and F. J. Barret (Eds) *The Masculinities Reader*. Cambridge: Polity

Benn, R., (1995) Higher Education: Non-Standard Students and Withdrawals. *Journal of Further and Higher Education*, 19(3): pp3-12

Benton De Corse, C. and Vogtle, S. (1997) In a Complex Voice: the contradictions of male elementary teachers' career choice and professional identity. *Journal of Teacher Education*, 48: pp37-46

Berger, P. (1963) *Invitation to Sociology: A Humanistic Perspective*. Harmondsworth: Penguin

Bernstein, B. (1972) Education Cannot Compensate for Society, in D. Rubenstein and C. Stoneman (Eds) *Education for Democracy*. Harmondsworth: Penguin

Biddulph, S. (1997) *Raising Boys*. Lane Cove, Australia: Finch Publishing

Biskup, C., Pfister, G. (1999) I would like to be like her/him: are athletes role-models for boys and girls? *European Physical Education Review*, 5(3): pp199-218

Bloom, A. (2005) Teachers forced to become assistants. *Times Educational Supplement*, 10th June 2005, p3

Board of Education, *Statistics of Public Education*, Reports to Parliament for the Board of Education, 1900-1944, London: Board of Education

Bonner, C. (1997) *What about the boys? Masculinity, Schools and Principals*. Australia: New South Wales Principals' Council

Botcherby, S. and Hurrell, K. (2004) *Ethnic minority women and men*, Equal Opportunities Commission, December 2004, London: EOC

Bourdieu, P. and Passeron, J. C. (1977) *Reproduction in Education: Society and Culture*. London: Sage

Bourner, T., Reynolds, A., Hamed, M. and Barnett, R., (1991) *Part-Time Students and their Experience of Higher Education*. Oxford: Oxford University Press

Bower, C. (2001) Trends in Female Employment, *Labour Market Trends*: pp93-106

Bowers, T. and Mciver, M. (2000), *Ill Health Retirement and Absenteeism Amongst Teachers, Research Brief No. 235*. London: Department for Education and Employment

Bowlby, J. (1953) *Child Care and the Growth of Love*. London: Pelican Books

Bradley, H. (1993) Across the Great Divide: The Entry of Men into 'Women's Jobs', pp11-27, in C. L. Williams (Ed) *Doing 'Women's Work': Men in Non-Traditional Occupations*. London: Sage

Bricheno, P. (2001) Pupil attitudes: a longitudinal study of children's attitudes to science at transfer from primary to secondary school. Unpublished PhD thesis, University of Greenwich

Bricheno, P. and Thornton, M. (2002) Staff Gender Balance in Primary Schools. *Research in Education*, 68: pp57-64

Bricheno, P. and Thornton, M. (2005) Role Models Revisited, a paper presented at the European Conference on Educational Research, University College Dublin, Ireland, September 2004

Bromnick, R. and Swallow, B. (1999) I like being who I am: A study of young people's ideals. *Educational Studies*, 2: pp117-128

Brookhart, S. M. and Loadman, W. E. (1996) Characteristics of male elementary teachers in the USA at teacher education program entry and exit. *Teaching and Education*, 12 (2): pp197-210.

Brutsaert, H. and Bracke, P. (1994) Gender context of the elementary school: sex differences in affective outcomes. *Educational Studies*, 20(1): pp3-11

Budge, D. (1999) Women lead in headship stakes, *Times Educational Supplement*, 15th October 1999, p1

Bunting, C. (2000) Stress on the emotional landscape. *Times Educational Supplement*, 10th November 2000, p23

Burn, E. (1998) The Boys Follow me Around, a paper presented at the British Educational Research Association Annual Conference, Belfast, September 1998

Bush, A, Edwards, L, Hopwood Road, F and Lewis, M (2005) Why here? Report of qualitative work with teachers working in schools above and below the floor targets, part of the IPPR *Choice and Equity in Teacher Supply* research project May 2005

Callaghan, J. (1976) Speech made at Ruskin College, *Times Educational Supplement*, 22 October 1976

Cameron, D. (2000) *Good to talk: living and working in a communication culture*, London: Sage

Campbell, R. J. and Neill, S. R. (1994) *Primary Teachers at Work*, London: Routledge

Carrington, B. (2002) A Quintessentially Feminine Domain? Student Teachers' Constructions of Primary Teaching as a Career. *Educational Studies*, 28 (3): pp287-303.

Carrington, B., and Skelton, C., (2003) Re-thinking 'role models': equal opportunities in teacher recruitment in England and Wales. *Journal of Education Policy*, 18 (3): pp253-265

Carrington, B., Tymms, P., and Merrell, C. (2005) Role models, school improvement and the 'gender gap' – Do men bring out the best in boys and women the best in girls? A paper presented to the EARLI 2005 Conference, University of Nicosia

Casassus, B. (2000) Female staff call for state support, *Times Higher Education Supplement*, 18th August 2000, p10

Case, J. (2005) Alienation and Engagement: Empirical evaluation of an alternative theoretical framework for understanding student learning, a paper presented at the Staff and Educational Development Association (SEDA) Spring Conference, Belfast, N. Ireland, 12-13 May

Central Statistical Office (1990) *Social Trends 20*. London: HMSO

Chambers, G. N. and Roper, T. (2000) Why Students Withdraw from Initial Teacher Training. *Journal of Education for Teaching*, 26 (1): pp25-43

Cheng, C (Ed) (1996) *Masculinities in Organisations*. London: Sage

Chung, T., Dolton, P. and Tremayne, A. (2004) *The Determinants of Teacher Supply: Time Series Evidence for the UK*, 1962-2001, Centre for Economic Performance, London School of Economics

Cockburn, C. (1983) *Brothers: male dominance and technological change.* London: Pluto Press

Cockburn, C. (1985) *Machinery of dominance: women, men, and technical know-how.* London: Pluto Press

Cockburn, C. (1991) *In the way of women: men's resistance to sex equality in organizations.* London: Macmillan

Cohen, M. (1998) 'A habit of healthy idleness': boys' underachievement in historical perspective, in D. Epstein, J. Elwood, V. Hey and J. Maw (Eds) *Failing Boys? Issues in gender and achievement.* Buckingham: Open University Press.

Cohen, N. (2005) The Death of Privacy, *The Observer*, 1st May 2005, p31

Coleman, M. (2002) *Women as Head Teachers: Striking the balance.* Stoke-on-Trent: Trentham Books

Colton, M. and Vanstone, M. (1996) *Betrayal of Trust: Sexual Abuse by men who work with children... in their own words.* London: Free Association Books

Connell, R. W. (1987) *Gender and Power. Society, the Person and Sexual Politics.* Cambridge: Polity Press

Connell, R. W. (1989) Cool Guys, Swots and Wimps: the interplay of masculinity and education, *Oxford Review of Education*, 15(3): pp291-303

Connell, R. W. (1995) *Masculinities.* Cambridge: Polity Press

Connell, R.W. (1982) *Making the Difference: Schools, Families and Social Division.* London: Allen and Unwin

Cooperative Insurance Society, (November 2001) *Teachers come top of the class as role models*, http://www.cis.co.uk.pages/news184.html

Copelman, D. M. (1996) *London's Women Teachers: Gender, Class, and Feminism, 1870-1930.* London: Routledge

Corrigan, P. (1979) *Schooling the Smash Street Kids.* London: Macmillan

Covington, M. (2000) Goal theory, Motivation and School Achievement: An integrative review, *Annual Review of Psychology*, 51, pp171-200

Cox, C.B. and Boyson, R. (1971) *The black papers on education.* London: Centre for Policy Studies

Cox, C.B. and Boyson, R. (1977) *Black Papers 1977*. London: Temple Smith.

Cox, C.B. and Dyson, A.E. (1969) *Fight for Education: a Black Paper*. London: Critical Quarterly

Cox, C.B. and Dyson, A.E. (1975) *Black paper*. London: Dent.

Croll, P., and Moses, D. (1990) Sex roles in the primary classroom, in C. Rogers and P. Kutnick (Eds) *The Social Psychology of the Primary School*. London: Routledge/Falmer

Cronin, H. (2005) Evolution, not sexism, puts us at a disadvantage in the sciences: The vital statistics, *The Guardian*, 12th March 2005: p21

Cubillo, L. (1999) Gender and leadership in the National Professional Qualification for Head Teachers: an opportunity lost? *Journal of In-Service Education*, 25 (3): pp545-556

Davidson, M. and Ferrario, M. (1992) A Comparative Study of Gender and Management Style, *Target-Management Review*, 5(1): pp13-17

Davies, L. (1984) *Pupil Power: Deviance and Gender in School*. London: Falmer Press

Davies, P., Mangan, J. and Telhaj, S. (2005), Bold, Reckless and Adaptable? Explaining gender differences in economic thinking and attitudes, *British Educational Research Journal*, 31 (1): pp29-48.

Dean. C. (2001) One man and his nursery: the government wants more men to break the mould and work in the early years, *Times Educational Supplement*, 13th April 2001, p12

Delamont, S. (1999) Gender and the Discourse of Derision, in *Research Papers in Education*, 14 (1): pp3-21

DES (1967) *Children and their Primary Schools: A report of the Central Advisory Council for Education (England) Volume 2: Research and Surveys*. Chairman Lady Plowden. London: HMSO

DES (1980) *A View of the Curriculum*. London: HMSO

DES (1981) *The School Curriculum*. London: HMSO

DES (1989) *The Education Reform Act 1988: The school curriculum and assessment, Circular No. 5/89*. London: HMSO

DES (1992) *Statistical Bulletin, Leaving rates amongst first year degree students in English polytechnics and colleges*. London: HMSO

DES/DfES, *Statistics of Education, 1961-2000*. London: HMSO

DfEE (2000), Boys Must Improve At Same Rate As Girls – Blunkett, *Press Notice 2000/0368* August 20th 2000, http://www.dfes.gov.uk/pns/DisplayPN.cgi?pn_id= 2000_0368

DfEE (1998) *Schools – achieving success*, White Paper. London: HMSO

DfEE, *Statistics of Education, 2000-2004*, Department for Education and Science, http://www.dfes.gov.uk/

DfES (1997) '*Playing for success*' http://www.dfes.gov.uk/playingforsuccess/

DfES (2004) *Statistics of Education. Schools in England 2004 Edition*. London: HMSO

DfES (2005a) *The Standards Site*, www.standards.dfes.gov.uk

DfES (2005b) *Time trend for O Level/GCSE attainment by gender*, 1962-2004, personal communication with M. Walker, DfES, July 15th, 2005

Dolton, P. and Chung, T-P, (2004) The rate of return to teaching: how does it compare to other graduate jobs, *National Institute Economic Review,* Number 190

Douglas, J.W.B., Ross, J.M., and Simpson, H.R., (1968) *All Our Future: A Longitudinal Study of Secondary Education.* London: Peter Davies

Drudy, S., Martin, M., Woods, M. and O'Flynn, J. (2005) *Men and the Classroom: gender imbalances in teaching.* London: Routledge Falmer

Durkheim, E. (1965) *The Division of Labor in Society.* New York: Free Press

Dweck, C., Davidson, W., Nelson, S. and Enna, B. (1978) Sex Differences in Learned Helplessness, *Developmental Psychology,* 14: pp268-276

Earnshaw, J., Ritchie, E., Marchington, L., Torrington, D. and Hardy, S. (2002) *Best Practice in Undertaking Teacher Capability Procedures Manchester School of Management UMIST, March 2002, Research Report RR312.* London: DfES

Eccles, J., Wigfield, A., Harold, R.D., and Blumenfield, P. (1993) Age and Gender Differences in Children's Self- and Task Perceptions during Elementary School. *Child Development,* 64 (3) pp830-47

Ecclestone, K. and Pryer, J. (2003) 'Learning Careers' or 'Assessment Careers'? The impact of Assessment Systems on Learning, *British Educational Research Journal,* 29(4): pp471-488

Education News, (2000) Parents and Teachers Top Teen Role Models, According to Junior Achievement/Harris Interactive Poll, http://www.educationnews.org/ Parents-and-Teachers-Top-Teen-Role-Models.htm

Edwards, S. and Lyons, G. (1994) Female secondary headteachers – and endangered species? *Management in Education,* 8(2): pp7-10

Edwards, S. and Lyons, G. (1996) It's grim up north for female high flyers, *Times Educational Supplement School Management Guide,* 10th May 1996, p2

Edwards, T., Power, S., Whitty, G. and Wigfall, V. (1998) Destined for Success? Academic ability and career trajectories, a paper presented at the British Educational Research Association Annual Conference, The Queen's University, Belfast, August 1998

Ehrenberg, R.G., Goldhaber, D.D., and Brewer, D.J., (1995) Do teachers' race, gender, and ethnicity matter? Evidence from the National Educational Longitudinal Study of 1988, *Industrial and Labor Relations Review,* 48, pp. 547-561.

Elton, R. E. (1989) *Discipline in Schools: report of the Committee of Enquiry chaired by Lord Elton.* London, HMSO

Emery, H. (1997) Men into Primary Teaching, *British Journal of Curriculum and Assessment,* 7 (2): pp35-37

Employers' Organisation for Local Government (2004) *Survey of Teacher Resignations and Recruitment 1885/6 -2002.* London: Employers' Organisation

Epstein, D. (1997) Boyz' own story: masculinities and sexualities in schools, *Gender and Education,* 9 (11): p105-116.

Equal Opportunities Commission (2005) *Facts About Women and Men in Great Britain 2005,* January, EOC (ISBN 1 84206 126 7) available at www.eoc.org.uk

ERA see DES (1989) *The Education Reform Act 1988: The school curriculum and assessment, Circular No. 5/89,* London: HMSO

Evetts, J. (1989) Primary Teachers' Careers: the contexts of expansion and contraction, *Cambridge Journal of Education,* 19 (3): pp287-297

Fidler, B., Earley, P., Ouston, J., and Davies, J.(1998) Teacher Gradings and Ofsted Inspections: help or hindrance as a management tool? *School Leadership and Management,* 18(2), pp.257-270

Finlayson, L.R. and Nazroo, J.Y. (1998) *Gender Inequalities in Nursing Careers.* London: Policy Studies Institute

Fitz-Gibbon, C.T and Stephenson-Forster, N.J. (1999) Is Ofsted helpful? Chapter 5, p97-118, in C. Cullingford (Ed.) *An Inspector Calls.* London: Kogan

Fitz-Gibbon, C.T. (1996) *Monitoring Education: Indicators, Quality and Effectiveness.* London: Cassell

Flintoff, A. (1993) One of the Boys? Gender Identities in Physical Education. Initial teacher Education, p74-93 in I. Siraj-Blatchford (Ed) *Race, Gender and the Education of Teachers.* Buckingham: Open University Press

Floge, L. and Merrill, D.M. (1986) Tokenism reconsidered: male nurses and female physicians in a hospital setting, *Social Forces,* 64: pp952-47

Foster, T. (1995) You don't have to be Female to Succeed on this Course, but it helps, *The Redland Papers,* Bristol, University of the West of England, Autumn, 35-43

Foster, T. and Newman, E. (2001a) 'The heart-ache and the thousand natural shocks that flesh is heir to': Bruising on the route to identity for male primary school teachers, a paper presented at the British Educational Research Association Annual Conference, Leeds, September 2001

Foster, T. and Newman, E. (2001b) Men, Mentoring and Masculinity: The Role of Mentoring in the Recruitment of Young Men into Primary Teaching, Paper presented to the Teacher Supply and Retention Conference, University of North London, June 12th

Francis B. (1998) *Power Plays: primary school children's constructions of gender, power and adult work.* Stoke-on-Trent: Trentham Books

Francis, B. (2000) *Boys, Girls and Achievement: Addressing the Classroom Issues.* London: Routledge/ Falmer.

Francis, B. and Skelton, C. (2001) Men Teachers and the construction of heterosexual masculinity in the classroom, *Sex Education,* 1 (1): pp1-17

Fredricks J.A. and Eccles J. S. (2002) Children's Competence and Value Beliefs from Childhood through Adolescence: Growth Trajectories in Two Male-Sex-Typed Domains, *Developmental Psychology,* 38(4): pp519-33

Frith, U. (1989) *Autism: Explaining the Enigma.* Oxford: Blackwell

Furedi, F. (2000) An unsuitable job for a man, *The Independent,* 12th October 2000: p5

Galton, M., Gray, J., and Rudduck, J. (1999) *The impact of school transitions and transfers on pupil progress and attainment. Research Report No. 131.* London: Department for Education and Employment

Gates, N. (1999) Undergraduate Teacher Training – A case of terminal decline?, *SCETT News,* Autumn, 2, pp4-5

Geake, J. (2005) Educational Neuroscience and Neuroscientific Education: in search of a mutual middle-way, *Research Intelligence,* 92, British Educational Research Association

Gillborn, D., and Gipps, C. (1996) *Recent Research on the Achievements of Ethnic Minority Pupils,* London: HMSO

Gipps, C. and Murphy, P. (1994) *A Fair Test: assessment, achievement and equity.* Buckingham: Open University Press.

Goddard, A. (2005) Female heads big winners in pay stakes, *Times Higher Educational Supplement,* 25th February 2005, p1

Gold, D. and Reis, M. (1982) Male teacher effects on young children: a theoretical and empirical consideration, *Sex Roles,* 8 (5): pp493-513

Goldberg, P.A. (1968) Are women prejudiced against women? *Transactions,* April 28-30

Gorard, S., and Taylor, C. (2001) *Measuring Markets: the case of the ERA 1988. Working paper 38. A preliminary consideration of the impact of market forces on educational standards.* Cardiff University School of Social Sciences

Gorman, T., White, J., Brooks, G., Maclure, M. and Kispal, A. (1988) *Language performance in schools: review of APU language monitoring 1979-1983.* London: HMSO

Gray, J. and Wilcox, B. (1995) The methodologies of school inspection: issues and dilemmas, in T. Brighouse and R. Moon (Eds) *School Inspection.* London: Pitman

GTC England (2000) *National Opinion Poll of Public Perceptions of Schools and Teachers,* DfES, London

GTC England (2003) Survey of Teachers' Opinions, (*The Guardian*/ MORI poll), January 2003

Hadow Report (1926) *Report of the Consultative Committee of the Board of Education on The Education of the Adolescent.* London: HMSO

Halpin, T. (2005) Secondary Schools lose 40% of their staff a year, *The Times,* 27th May 2005, p29

Hargreaves, A. (1967) *Social Relations in a Secondary School.* London: Routledge and Kegan-Paul

Hargreaves, L., Maddock, M. and Turner, P. (2004) The Status of Teachers and the Teaching profession, a paper presented at the European Conference on Educational Research, University of Crete at Rethymnon, Crete, September 2004, (with leader author's permission to quote)

Harnett, P. (2003) Where have all the men gone? Have primary schools really been feminised? *Journal of Educational Administration and History,* 35(2): pp77-86

Hastings, S. (2005) Headship, *Times Educational Supplement,* 14th October 2005, p11-14

Health and Safety Executive (2000) *The scale of occupational stress: A further analysis of the impact of demographic factors and type of job,* Centre for Occupational and Health Psychology School of Psychology, Cardiff University for the Health and Safety Executive. Website: http://www.hse.gov.uk/

Health and Safety Executive (2004) Psychosocial Working Conditions in Great Britain in 2004, Health and Safety Executive March 2004. http://www.hse.gov.uk/

Henry, J. Boys outshine girls at the highest level, *Times Educational Supplement,* Aug.23rd, 2002, p1

Hicks, J. and Allen, G. (1999) *A Century of Change: Trends in UK Statistics since 1900,* Research Paper 99/111, 21st December 1999, House of Commons Library

Hill, A. (2005) Childcare shake-up will send men into the nursery, *The Observer,* 6th March 2005: p7

Hinsliff, G. and Tenko, N. (2005) *The Observer,* 3rd July 2005, p.13

HMI, (1978) *Primary Education in England: A Survey by HM Inspectors of Schools.* London: HMSO

Hoel, H. and Cooper, C.L. (2000) *Destructive Conflict and Bullying at Work,* Sponsored by the British Occupational Health Research Foundation, Manchester School of Management, University of Manchester Institute Science and Technology (UMIST) November, 2000, extracts of study report compiled for Launch of the Civil Service Race Equality Network (September, 2001)

HON News (2003) Eat as I eat, *Health on the Net Forum,* May 2003, http://www.hon.ch/News/HSN/513161.html

Hooton, L. (1997) *Selection – Indications of Outcome?* Glasgow: Caledonian University

Hopf, D., and Hatzichristou, C. (1999) Teacher gender-related influences in Greek schools, *British Journal of Educational Psychology,* 69(1): pp1-18

House of Commons (1997) *Education and Employment, First Report: Session 1997-1998, Section C: Quality of ITT students and those entering teaching,* p1-5 28th October, 1997:1, Norwich: The Stationery Office or http://www. parliament. the-stationery-office.co.uk/pa/cm199798/cmselect/cmeduemp/262i/ee0102. htm

House of Commons Education and Skills Committee (2004) *Secondary Education: Teacher Retention and Recruitment. Fifth Report of Session 2003-04. Volumes I and II.* HC 1057-1 and HC 1057-11. London: The Stationery Office

Howe, C. (1997) *Gender and Classroom Interaction: A Resarch Review.* Edinburgh: Scottish Council for Research in Education

Huggins, M., and Knight, P. (1997) Curriculum continuity and transfer from primary to secondary school: the case of history, *Educational Studies,* 23(3): pp333-348

Hutchings, M. (2002) A representative profession? Gender issues, in M. Johnson and J. Hallgarten (Eds.) *From Victims of Change to Agents of Change: The Future of the Teaching Profession.* London: Institute for Public Policy Research

Hutchings, M., Menter, I., Ross, A. and Thomson, D. (2002) Teacher supply and retention in London: Key findings and implications from a study carried out in six London boroughs in 1998 – 2000, in I. Menter, M. Hutchings and A. Ross (Eds.) *The Crisis in Teacher Supply: Research and Strategies for Retention.* Stoke-on-Trent: Trentham

Jackson, C. (2003) Motives for 'Laddishness' at School: fear of failure and fear of the feminine, *British Educational Research Journal,* 29 (4): pp583-598

Jacobs, J. (1993) Men in Female-Dominated Fields, pp49-63 in C.L. Williams *Doing Women's Work: Men in nontraditional occupations.* Newbury Park, CA: Sage

Johnes, J. and Taylor, J. (1989) Undergraduate on-completion rates: Differences between UK universities, *Higher Education,* 18(1): pp209-225

Johnes, J. (1990) Determinants of Student Wastage in Higher Education, *Studies in Higher Education,* 15(1): pp87-99

Johnston, J., McKeown, E., and McEwan, A. (1998) *Gender Factors in Choosing Primary School Teaching.* Northern Ireland: Equal Opportunities Commission.

Johnston, J., McKeown, E. and McEwen, A. (1999) Choosing Primary Teaching as a Career: the perspectives of males and females in training, *Journal of Education for Teaching*, 25(1): pp55-64

Jones, M.L. (1990) The Attitudes of Men and Women Primary School Teachers to Promotion and Educational Management, *Educational Management and Administration*, 18(3): pp11-16

Jones, S. (2003) *The Descent of Men*. Boston: Houghton Mifflin

Jules, V. and Kutnick, P. (1997) Student perceptions of a good teacher: the gender perspective, *British Journal of Educational Psychology*, 67: pp497-511

Junior Achievement (2003) Teens List Parents as Their Top Role Models, *Junior Achievement/ Harris Interactive Poll, 2003*, http://www.ja.org/about/about_newsitem.asp?StoryID=122http://www.ja.org/about/about_newsitem.asp?StoryID=122

Kaufman, M. (1994) Men, Feminisation and Men's Contradictory Experiences of power, pp142-164 in H. Brod and M. Kaufman (Eds) *Theorising Masculinities*. Thousand Oaks, CA: Sage

Kauppinen-Toropainen, K. and Lammi, J. (1993) Men in Female Dominated Occupations: A Cross-Cultural Comparison, in C. L. Williams (Ed.) *Doing 'Women's Work': Men in Non-Traditional Occupations*. London: Sage

Kenway, J. and Willis, S. (1998) *Answering Back*. London: Routledge

Keys, W., Harris, S. and Fernandes C. (1995) *Attitudes to school of top primary and first-year secondary pupils*. Slough: NFER

Kimmel, M.S. (1994) Masculinity as Homophobia: Fear, shame and silence in the construction of gender identity, pp119-141 in H. Brod and M. Kaufman (Eds) *Theorizing Masculinities*. London: Sage

Klein, U. (1999) Our best boys: The Gendered nature of civil-military relations in Israel, *Men and Masculinities*, 2(1): pp47-65

Kohlberg, L.A. (1966) A Cognitive development analysis of children's sex role concepts and attitudes, pp82-173 in E.E. Maccoby (Ed) *The Development of Sex Difference*, London: Tavistock

Lacey, C. (1970) *Hightown Grammar*. Manchester: Manchester University Press

Lahelma, A. (2000) Lack of male teachers: a problem for students or teachers? *Pedagogy, Culture and Society*, 8(2): pp173-185

Laurance, J. (2004) Medical time-bomb: too many women doctors, *The Independent*, 2nd August 2004, p1

Lawton, D. (1982) *The End of the 'Secret Garden'? A Study in the Politics of the Curriculum*. London, University of London Institute of Education

Lee, J. and Slater, J. (2005) Old boys' club of private headship, *Times Educational Supplement*, 14th January, p.5

Lepkowska, D. (2005) Why girls don't tap into plumbing, *Times Educational Supplement*, 15th July 2005, p14.

Lewis, P. (2002) An enquiry into male drop-out rate on a PGCE primary course at a university college and success indicators for retention, pp123-137 in *The Crisis in Teacher Supply* ed. Menter, I. Hutchings, M. and Ross, A., Stoke on Trent: Trentham Books

Loizou, C.D. and Rossiter, D. (1987) *The Role of the Mathematics Post-Holder in Primary School*. Birmingham: University of Birmingham

Lynch, K. (1994) Women Teach and Men Manage: Why men dominate senior posts in Irish education, *Women for Leadership in Education*, Conference of Religious of Ireland, Dublin: Milltown Park

Mac An Ghaill, M. (1994) *The Making of Men: Masculinities, Sexualities and Schooling*. Buckingham: Open University Press

MacDonald, I. (1992) Meeting the needs of non-traditional students: challenge or opportunity for higher education, *Scottish Journal of Adult Education*, 1(2), pp34-44

Mackay, C., Cousins, R., Kelly, P.J., Lee, S. and McCaig, R.H. (2004) 'Management Standards' and work-related stress in the UK: Policy background and science, *Work and Stress*, 18(2), pp91-112

Mahony, P. and Hextall, I. (2000) *Reconstructing Teaching: Standards, performance and accountability*. London: Routledge Falmer

Mahony, P., Menter, I. and Hextall, I. (2004a) The Emotional Impact of Threshold Assessment on Teachers in England, *British Education Research Journal*, 30(3): pp443-464

Mahony, P., Menter, I. and Hextall, I. (2004b) Threshold Assessment and performance management: modernizing or masculinising teaching? *Gender and Education*, 16(2): pp131-149

Malderez, A., Hobson, A.J., Kerr, K., Tracey, L. and Pell, G. (2004) *Why Train to Teach? Comparing the motives of trainees following six different routes into teaching in England: early findings from the Becoming a Teacher Project*, a paper presented at the European Conference on Educational Research, University of Crete at Rethymnon, Crete, September 2004

Mancus, D. S. (1992) Influence of Male Teachers on Elementary School Children's Stereotyping of Teacher Competence, *Sex Roles*, 26 (3-4): pp109-128

Mansell, W. (2000) 'Ladies' job' tag deters recruits, *Times Education Supplement*, 14th January, p1

Martin, A. and Marsh, H. (2005) Motivating boys, motivating girls: Does teacher gender really make a difference? *Australian Journal of Education*, 49 (3) pp 320-334

Martinez, P., and Munday, F. (1998) *9,000 Voices: student persistence and drop-out in further education*. London: FEDA

McAvoy, D. (2000) Education Degree Prejudice, *Times Education Supplement*, 9th June 2000, p23

McBeath, J. and Galton, M. (2004) Finding time to teach, *Managing Schools Today*, 13(6): pp35-37

McKie, R. and Harris, P. (2005) A woman's place... is not at Harvard, *The Observer*, 6th March 2005, p18

McNair Report (1944) The McNair Report cited p.216-221 J. S. Maclure, *Educational Documents: England and Wales 1816-1967*, London: Chapman and Hall

Measor, L. and Sikes, P. (1992) *Gender and schools*. London: Cassell

Mills, M. (2000) Issues in Implementing Boys' Programme in Schools: male teachers and empowerment, *Gender and Education*, 12(2): pp221-238

Mills, M. (2005) The Male Teacher Debate Australian Style: The Catholic Education Office (CEO) vs Human Rights and Equal Opportunities Commission

(HREOC), a paper presented at the Graduate School of Education, Queen's University, Belfast, 6th May

Ministry of Education, *Statistics of Education*, Reports to Parliament, Education, 1944-1964, Ministry of Education. London: HMSO

Moir, A. and Moir, B. (1998) *Why Men Don't Iron: The Real Science of Gender Studies*. London: Harper Collins

Moore, R. (2000) For Knowledge: tradition, progressivism and progress in education – reconstructing the curriculum debate, *Cambridge Journal of Education*, 30(2): pp17-36

MORI (2001) *Evidence Gathering – Issues in the Recruitment and Retention of Teachers*, Qualitative Research Research Study Conducted for The General Teaching Council September 2001. London: MORI

MORI (2002) *Teachers on Teaching A Survey of the Teaching Profession*, Research Study Conducted for The General Teaching Council (with PR21 and the Guardian) October-November 2002. London: MORI

Moyles, J. and Cavendish, S. (2001) Male students in primary ITT: a failure to thrive, strive or survive? A paper presented at the British Educational Research Association Annual Conference, Leeds University, 13-15 September 2001, http://www.leeds.ac.uk /educol/documents/00001908.htm, 2001, pp. 17.

Munn, P., Johnstone, M. and Holligan, C. (1990) Pupils' perceptions of 'effective disciplinarians', *British Education Research Journal*, 16 (2): pp191-198

Murdoch, A. (1986) Forty-two children and the transfer to secondary education, in M. Youngman (Ed) *Mid-Schooling Transfer: Problems and Proposals*. Windsor: NFER-Nelson

Murphy, P., and Elwood, J. (1998) Gendered learning outside and inside school: influences on achievement, pp162-181 in Epstein, D., Elwood, J., Hay, V., and Maw, J. (Eds) *Failing Boys? Issues in Gender and Achievement*. Buckingham: Open University Press

NASUWT (1996) *No Place to Hide: Confronting Workplace Bullies*. Birmingham: NASUWT

National Reading Campaign, (accessed on 03/08/03) http://www.literacytrust.org.uk/Pubs/Footyindex.html

National Union of Teachers (1999) *Tackling Stress*: National Union of Teachers, Health and Safety Briefing

Nias, J. (1987) Teaching and the Self, *Cambridge Journal of Education*, 17(3): pp178-185

Nias, J. (1989) *Primary Teachers Talking*. New York: Penguin

Nickell, S. and Quintini, G. (2002) The consequences of the decline in public sector pay in Britain: A little bit of evidence, *Economic Journal*, 112, pp.F107-F118

NLT (National Literacy Trust), (2003) *Sporting Heroes Join the Campaign*, http://www.literacytrust.org.uk

Noble, C. (1998) Helping boys do better in their primary schools, in K. Bleach, (Ed) *Raising Boys' Achievement in Schools*. Stoke on Trent: Trentham Books

North, M. (2005) Too cool for school and it's downhill from there, *Times Higher Education Supplement*, 25th February 2005, p21

Ofsted (2002) *The Graduate Teacher Programme (HMI 346)*. London: The Stationery Office

Ofsted (2003a) *Flexible postgraduate initial teacher training (HMI 1766)*. London: The Stationery Office www.ofsted.gov.uk

Ofsted (2003b) *An evaluation of the Training Schools programme (HMI 1769)*. London: The Stationery Office www.ofsted.gov.uk

Ofsted (2005a) The CD-ROM accompanying *the Annual Report of Her Majesty's Chief Inspector of Schools 2003/04 Summary*. London: The Stationery Office, http://www.ofsted.gov.uk/publications/index.cfm?fuseaction=pubs.summarya ndid=3829

Ofsted (2005b) *Using the evaluation schedule Guidance for inspectors of schools*. London: The Stationery Office. www.ofsted.gov.uk

Ofsted (2005c) *An employment-based route into teaching: An overview of the first year of the inspection of designated recommended bodies for the Graduate Teacher Programme 2003/04 (HMI 2406)*. London: The Stationery Office. Website: www.ofsted.gov.uk

Opinion (2002) *Times Educational Supplement*, 13th September, 2002, p.22

Oram, A. (1989) A Master Should Not Serve Under a Mistress: Women and Men Teachers 1900-1970, in S. Acker (Ed) *Teachers, Gender and Careers*. Lewes: Falmer Press

Oram, A. (1996) *Women Teachers and Feminist Politics, 1900-1939*. Manchester: Manchester University Press

Osler, A. and Vincent, K. (2003) *Girls and Exclusion: rethinking the agenda*. London: Routledge Falmer

Owen, C., Cameron, C. and Moss, P. (Eds) (1998) *Men as Workers in Services for Young Children: Issues of a Mixed Gender Workforce*, Bedford Way Papers. London: Institute of Education, University of London

Ozga, J. and Sukhnandan, L. (1998) Undergraduate non-completion: developing an explanatory model. *Higher Education Quarterly*, 52(3): pp316-333

Paechter, C. (1998) *Educating the Other: Gender, Power and Schooling*. London, Harper Collins

Parry, (2005) Teach at first, but then move on, *Times Educational Supplement*, 8th July 2005, p13

Partington, G. (1976) *Women Teachers in the Twentieth century in England and Wales*. Windsor: NFER

Paton, G. and Lee, J. (2005) Premiership pitches in with BTec, *Times Educational Supplement*, 29th April 2005, p6

Penn H. and Mcquail, S. (1997) *Childcare as a Gendered Occupation*, DfEE Research Report 22. London: HMSO

Phillips, M. (2002) The feminisation of education, *The Daily Mail*, 19th August 2002

Phillips, S. (2005) At what point to weight the odds? *Times Higher Educational Supplement*, 25th February 2005, pp20-21

Phoenix, A. (2001) Racialisation and gendering in the (re)production of educational inequalities, pp126-138 in B. Francis and C. Skelton (Eds) *Investigating Gender: Contemporary perspectives in education*. Buckingham: Open University Press

Piper, H. and Smith, H. (2003) 'Touch' in Educational and Child-care Settings: dilemmas and responses, *British Educational Research Journal*, 29 (6): pp878-894

Powney, J., Wilson, V., Hall, S., Davidson, J., Kirk, S. and Edward, S. in conjunction with Mizra, H. S. (2003) *Teachers' Careers: the Impact of Age, Disability, Ethnicity, gender and Sexual Orientation (Research Report RR488)*. London: Department for Education and Skills.

Pye, D., Haywood, C. and Mac-an-Ghaill, M. (1996) The training state, de-industrialisation and the production of white working-class trainee identities. *International Studies in Sociology of Education*, 6(2): pp133-146

Pyke, N. (1998) Inspections get TV grilling, *Times Educational Supplement*, 20th March 1998, http://www.tes.co.uk/search/story/?story_id=303862

Reay, D. (2001) The paradox of contemporary femininities, pp152-163 in B. Francis and C. Skelton (Eds) *Investigating Gender: Contemporary Perspectives in Education*. Buckinghamshire: Open University Press

Reay, D. (2002) Shaun's Story: troubling discourses of white working-class masculinities, *Gender and Education*, 14 (3): pp221-234

Reid, I. and Thornton, M. (2000) *Students' Reasons for Choosing Primary School Teaching as a Career*. University of Hertfordshire, Centre for Equality Issues in Education, Aldenham

Rickinson, B. and Rutherford, D., (1995) Increasing undergraduate student retention rates, *British Journal of Guidance and Counselling*, 23: pp161-172

Riddell, S., Baron, S. and Wilson, A. (2001) Gender and the post-school experiences of women and men with learning difficulties, pp93-115 in B. Francis and C. Skelton (Eds) *Investigating Gender: Contemporary Perspectives in Education*. Buckingham: Open University Press

Ross, A. and Hutchings, M. (2003) *Attracting, Developing and Retaining Effective Teachers in the United Kingdom of Great Britain and Northern Ireland*. OECD Country Background Report. London: Institute for Policy Studies in Education, London Metropolitan University

Rutter, M. (2004) A conundrum of the sexes: Are the differences between men and women driven by genes, hormones or patterns of upbringing? *Times Higher Educational Supplement*, 1st October 2004, pp24-25

Ruxton, S. (1992) *What's he doing at the Family Centre*. London: National Children's Homes.

Ryan, A. M. and Pintrich, P.R. (1997) 'Should I Ask for Help?' The Role of Motivation and Attitudes in Adolescents' Help Seeking in Math Class, *Journal of Educational Psychology*, 89(2): pp329-41.

Sargent, P. (2000) Real Men or Real Teachers? Contradictions in the lives of Men Elementary Teachers, *Men and Masculinities*, 2 (4): 410-433

Sargent, P. (2001) *Real Men or Real Teachers? Contradictions in the Lives of Men Elementary School Teachers*. Harriman, Tennessee, USA: Men's Studies Press

Scott, C., Cox, S. and Gray, A. (1998) The State of the Profession: An English Study of Teacher Satisfaction, Motivation and Health, a paper presented at the British Educational Research Association Annual Conference, Belfast, 1998

Sharp, R. and Green, A. (1975) *Education and Social Control: A Study of Progressive Primary Education*. London: Routledge and Kegan Paul

Shaw, G.B. (1903) *Maxims for Revolutionists, in Man and Superman*. London: Penguin

Simpson, R. and Simpson, I. (1969) Women and Bureaucracy in the Semi-Professions, pp196-265 in A. Etzioni (Ed) *The Semi-Professions and Their Organisation*. New York: Free Press.

Skelton, C. (1987) A Study of Gender Discrimination in a primary programme of teacher training, *Journal of Education for Teaching*, 13 (2): pp163-175

Skelton, C. (1991) A Study of the Career Perspectives of Male Teachers of Young Children, *Gender and Education*, 3 (3): pp278-89

Skelton, C. (2001a) *Schooling the Boys: masculinities and primary schooling*. Buckingham: Open University Press

Skelton, C. (2001b) 'A passion for football': dominant masculinities and primary schooling, *Sport, Education and Society*, 5(1): pp 5-18

Skelton, C. (2002) The 'Feminisation of Schooling' or 'Remasculinising' Primary Education? *International Studies in Sociology of Education*, 12(1): pp77-96

Skelton, C. and Francis, B. (2001) Endnotes: gender, school policies and practice, pp189-195 in B. Francis and C. Skelton (Eds) *Investigating Gender: Contemporary perspectives in education*. Buckingham: Open University Press

Skelton, C. and Hanson, J. (1989) Schooling the teachers: Gender and initial teacher education, in S. Acker (Ed) *Teachers, Gender and Careers*. Lewes: Falmer Press

Slater, J. (2005) Boys do better in co-ed schools, *Times Educational Supplement*, 29th April 2005, p10

Smedley, S. (1997) Men on the Margins: Male Student Primary Teachers, *Changing English*, 4 (2): pp217-227

Smith, C. and Lloyd, B. (1978) Maternal Behaviour and perceived sex of infant: revisited, *Child Development*, 49: pp1263-5

Smithers, A. and Robinson, P. (2001) *Teachers Leaving*, University of Liverpool, Liverpool/ National Union of Teachers, London

Smithers, A. and Robinson, P. (2003) *Factors Affecting Teachers' Decisions to Leave the Profession. Research Report 430*. London: DfES

Smithers, A. and Robinson, P. (2004) *Teacher Turnover, Wastage and Destinations. Research Report 553*. London: DfES

Smithers, A. and Robinson, P. (2005) *Teacher Turnover, Wastage and Movements between Schools. Research Report 640*. London: DfES

Southworth, G. (1990) *Staff selection in the primary school*. Oxford: Joshua Associates

Spear, M., Gould, K. and Lee, B. (2000) *Who Would be a Teacher? A Review of Factors Motivating and Demotivating Prospective and Practising Teachers*. Slough: National Foundation for Educational Research

Spelman, B.J. (1979) *Pupil Adaptation to Secondary School*. Belfast: The Northern Ireland Council for Educational Research

St. John-Brooks, C. (2001) What they want is a little respect, *Times Educational Supplement*, 7th September 2001, pp26-27

Stake, J.E. and Katz, J.F. (1982) Teacher-pupil relationships in the elementary school classroom: teacher-gender and pupil gender differences, *American Educational Research Journal*, 19(3): pp465-471

Steedman, C. (1985) 'The Mother made Conscious': The historical development of primary school pedagogy, *History Workshop Journal*, 20: pp149-63

Stewart, W. and Lucas, S. (2005) Rebellion simmers over pay, *Times Educational Supplement*, 24th June 2005, p3.

Stone, M. (1981) *The Education of the Black Child in Britain: the myth of multi-racial education*. London: Fontana.

Sturman, L. (2002) *Contented and Committed? A Survey of Quality of Working Life Amongst Teachers*. Slough: National Foundation for Educational Research.

Sturman, L., Lewis, K., Morrison, J., Scott, E., Smith, P., Styles, B., Taggart G. and Woodthorpe, A. (2005) *National Foundation for Educational Research General Teaching Council Survey of Teachers Final Report*, June 2005

Szabo, A. and Underwood, J. (2004) Cybercheats: Is information and communication technology fuelling academic dishonesty? *Active Learning in Higher Education*, 5 (2): pp180-199.

Teacher Development Agency (2005) Annual report and financial statements 2004-05 http://www.tda.gov.uk/about/planspoliciesreports/reports/annual report20042005.aspx

Teacher Development Agency (2005) General Information (Applying for Training) http://www.tda.gov.uk/partners/careersadvisers/applying/general information.aspx

Teacher Training Agency (2003)Annual Report 2002-2003, http://www.tda. gov.uk/about/planspoliciesreports/reports/annualreport20042005/archivedan nualreports.aspx

Teacher Training Agency (2004) Annual Report and Financial Statement 2003-2004, http://www.tda.gov.uk/about/planspoliciesreports/reports/annualreport 20042005/archivedannualreports.aspx

THES (2005) News in Brief, 'Only the boys boot up' *Times Higher Education Supplement* 2005:6, May 13th

Thomas-Scott, L. (2000) Ties that Bind: A Social Network Approach To Understanding Student Integration and Persistence, *Journal of Higher Education*, 71(5): pp591-615.

Thornton, K. (2000b) A new beginning, *Times Educational Supplement*, 20th October 2000, p29.

Thornton, K. (2001) Job or partner? Why, when it comes to headship, are so many women forced to choose? *Times Educational Supplement* Friday, 8th October 2001, pp8-9.

Thornton, K. (2003) Fast-track overtaken by alternative leaders scheme, *Times Educational Supplement*, 17th January 2003, p12

Thornton, M. (1995) Primary Teachers and the Primary Curriculum, *New Era in Education*, 76(3): pp78-83

Thornton, M. (1996) Subject Specialism, Gender and Status: The Example of Primary School Mathematics, *Education 3-13*, 24(3): pp53-54

Thornton, M. (1998) *Subject Specialists – Primary Schools, UCET Occasional Paper Number 10*. London: Universities Council for the Education of Teachers

Thornton, M. (1999a) Men into primary teaching: Who goes where? Dilemmas of entry, survival and career prospects, *Education 3-13*, June: pp50-56

Thornton, M. (1999b) Reducing Wastage among Men Student Teachers in Primary Courses: a male club approach, *Journal of Education for Teaching*, 25(1): pp41-53

Thornton, M. (2000a) Male Students on Primary Initial Teacher Education Courses, pp70-84 in S. Shah (Ed) *Equality Issues for the New Millennium*. Aldershot: Ashgate Press

Thornton, M. and Bricheno, P. (2000) Primary Teachers Careers in England and Wales: the relationship between gender, role, position and promotion aspirations, *Pedagogy, Culture and Society*, 8(2): pp187-206

Thornton, M. and Reid, I. (2001) Primary Teacher Recruitment: Careers Guidance and Advice, *Education 3-13*, 29(2): pp49-54

Thornton, M., Bricheno, P. and Reid, I. (2002) Students' reasons for wanting to teach in primary school, *Research in Education*, 67: p33-43

Tinklin, T. (2003) Gender Differences in High Attainment, *British Journal of Educational Research*, 29 (3): pp307-325

Tinklin, T., Croxford, L., Ducklin, A. and Frame, B. (2001) *Gender and pupil performance in Scotland's schools*. Edinburgh: The Scottish Executive Education Department

Tinto, V. (1993) *Leaving College: Rethinking the Causes and Cures of Student Attrition (2nd Edition)*. Chicago: The University of Chicago Press

TTA (2002) Corporate Plan 2002-05 http://www.canteach.gov.uk

Ul-Haq, R., Stiles, J. and Pond, K. (2003) Learning Expectations and learning Process design, *Active Learning in Higher Education*, 4 (2): pp168-180.

Van Ijzendoorn, M.H., Juffer, F. and Klein Poelhuis, C.W. (2005) Adoption and cognitive development: A meta-analytic comparison of adopted and non-adopted children's IQ and school performance, *Psychological Bulletin*, 131(2): pp301-316.

Vescio, J. A., Crosswhite, J. J. and Wilde, K. (2004) The impact of gendered heroism on adolescent girls and their sport role models, a paper presented at the Pre-Olympic Congress, International Congress on Sport Science, Sport Medicine and Physical Education, Thessaloniki, August 2004

Walkerdine, V. (1998) *Counting Girls Out*, (2nd edition) London: Falmer Press

Waller, W. (1965) *The Sociology of Teaching*. New York: J.Wiley and Sons

Ward, H. (2001) Quality of males takes a nose dive, *Times Educational Supplement*, 19th October 2001, p2

Warren, L. (1997) The career structure of women in education, *Irish Educational Studies*, 16, pp69-84

Weale, S, (1996) Hooray, hooray for equal pay, *The Guardian*, 28th March 1996: p6

Weinberg, R. S., Gould, D. and Jackson, A. (1979). Expectations and performance: An empirical test of Bandura's self-efficacy theory. *Journal of Sport Psychology*, 1: pp320-331

Whitelaw, S., Milosevic, L. and Daniels, S. (2000) Gender, behaviour and achievement: a preliminary study of pupil perceptions and attitudes, *Gender and Education*, 12(1): pp87-113

Whittaker, M. (2002) Where are all the men? *Times Educational Supplement*, 21st June 2002, pp19-20

Whyte, J. (1984) Observing sex stereotypes and interactions in the school lab and workshop, *Educational Review,* 36 (1): pp75-86

Whyte, J. (1986) *Girls into science and technology: the story of a project.* London: Routledge and Kegan Paul

Wilce, H. (2002) Looking for Mr Right, *Times Educational Supplement,* 6th December 2002, p8-9

Wilder, G. and Powell, K. (1989) *Sex differences in test performance: a survey of the literature.* New York: College Board Publications

Wilkins, R and Head, M. (2002) *How to Retain and Motivate Experienced Teachers.* Canterbury: Christ Church University College Centre for Education Leadership and School Improvement

Williams, C. L. and Villemez, W. J. (1993) Seekers and Finders: Male Entry or Exit in Female-Dominated Jobs, pp64-90 in C.L.Williams (Ed) *Doing Women's Work: Men in nontraditional occupation,* Newbury Park, CA: Sage

Williams, C.L. (2000) The Glass Escalator: Hidden Advantages for Men in the 'Female' Professions, in M. S. Kimmel (Ed) with A. Aronson, *The Gendered Society.* Oxford: Oxford University Press

Williams, D. (2002) Gender dominates the school agenda. Primary educators seek male graduates, *The Guardian* May 18th, 2002, http://education.guardian.co.uk/teachershortage/story/0,7348,717547,00.html

Williams, E. and Jones, A. (2005) An Unprotected Species? On teachers as risky subjects, *British Educational Research Journal,* 31(1): pp109-120

Williams, P., (1980) Role-model identification and school achievement: a developmental study, a paper presented at the Annual Convention of the American Psychological Association, Montreal, Canada, Sept 1-5, 1980

Willis, P. (1977) Learning to Labour. Aldershot: Saxon House

Wilson, M. (1997) (Ed) *Women in Educational Management,* London: Chapman

Woodley, A., Thompson, M. and Cowan, J. (1992) Factors Affecting Non-Completion Rates in Scottish Universities, *SRC Report No.69*

Woods, P. and Carlyle, D. (2002) Teacher Identities Under Stress: the Emotions of Separation and Renewal, *International Studies of Sociology of Education,* 12 (2): pp169-189

Woodward, R. (1998) 'It's a man's life!': Soldiers, Masculinity and the Countryside, *Gender, Place and Culture: A Journal of Feminist Geography,* 5(3): pp277-301.

Wragg, E.C., Haynes, G.S., Wragg, C.M. and Chamberlin, R.P. (2000) *Failing Teachers?* London: Routledge

Wylie, C. (2000) *Trends in feminization of the teaching profession in OECD countries 1980-95,* Working Papers, Geneva; International Labour Office, http://www.ilo.org/public/english/dialogue/sector/sectors/educat/publ.htm

Yorke, M. (1999) *Leaving Early: Undergraduate non-completion in higher education.* London: Falmer Press

Younger, M., Warrington, M., and Williams, J. (1999) The gender gap and classroom interactions: reality and rhetoric? *British Journal of Sociology of Education,* 20(3): pp325-341.

Zepke, N. and Leach, L. (2005) Integration and adaptation: Approaches to the student retention and achievement puzzle, *Active Learning in Higher Education,* 6(1): pp46-59

Index